FLOYD CLYMER'S MOTORCYCLIST'S LIBRARY

The Book of the
VILLIERS ENGINE

A General Guide to the operation and maintenance of single- and twin-cylinder Villiers two-stroke engines (deals with most current and earlier marks fitted to motor-cycles and other forms of transport)

Cyril Grange

ANNOUNCEMENT

By special arrangement with the original publishers of this book, Sir Isaac Pitman & Son, Ltd., of London, England, we have secured the exclusive publishing rights for this book, as well as all others in THE MOTORCYCLIST'S LIBRARY.

Included in THE MOTORCYCLIST'S LIBRARY are complete instruction manuals covering the care and operation of respective motorcycles and engines; valuable data on speed tuning, and thrilling accounts of motorcycle race events. See listing of available titles elsewhere in this edition.

We consider it a privilege to be able to offer so many fine titles to our customers.

FLOYD CLYMER
Publisher of Books Pertaining to Automobiles and Motorcycles

2125 W. PICO ST.   LOS ANGELES 6, CALIF.

INTRODUCTION

Welcome to the world of digital publishing ~ the book you now hold in your hand, while unchanged from the original edition, was printed using the latest state of the art digital technology. The advent of print-on-demand has forever changed the publishing process, never has information been so accessible and it is our hope that this book serves your informational needs for years to come. If this is your first exposure to digital publishing, we hope that you are pleased with the results. Many more titles of interest to the classic automobile and motorcycle enthusiast, collector and restorer are available via our website at www.VelocePress.com. We hope that you find this title as interesting as we do.

NOTE FROM THE PUBLISHER

The information presented is true and complete to the best of our knowledge. All recommendations are made without any guarantees on the part of the author or the publisher, who also disclaim all liability incurred with the use of this information.

TRADEMARKS

We recognize that some words, model names and designations, for example, mentioned herein are the property of the trademark holder. We use them for identification purposes only. This is not an official publication.

INFORMATION ON THE USE OF THIS PUBLICATION

This manual is an invaluable resource for the classic motorcycle enthusiast and a "must have" for owners interested in performing their own maintenance. However, in today's information age we are constantly subject to changes in common practice, new technology, availability of improved materials and increased awareness of chemical toxicity. As such, it is advised that the user consult with an experienced professional prior to undertaking any procedure described herein. While every care has been taken to ensure correctness of information, it is obviously not possible to guarantee complete freedom from errors or omissions or to accept liability arising from such errors or omissions. Therefore, any individual that uses the information contained within, or elects to perform or participate in do-it-yourself repairs or modifications acknowledges that there is a risk factor involved and that the publisher or its associates cannot be held responsible for personal injury or property damage resulting from the use of the information or the outcome of such procedures.

WARNING!

One final word of advice, this publication is intended to be used as a reference guide, and when in doubt the reader should consult with a qualified technician.

Preface

RIDING Villiers-engined motor-cycles for 45 years, starting with the Mark IV in 1922, confirms my experience that the Villiers is the best two-stroke engine on the market. No wonder then that total production to date is in excess of 3,000,000 engines, of which over 1,000,000 are two-stroke units for motor-cycles.

Without doubt, Villiers "two-strokes" are remarkable for their low capital cost, economy in operation and freedom from trouble. Not only have they proved themselves for general utility purposes but also for trials work, scrambling, racing, and for invalid carriages, etc.

That the firm's designers are in the top rank must be conceded when we study the most modern developments of the combined engine-gear unit, the electric starter, the cowled blower and the flywheel-ignition-lighting assembly.

This book, brought up to date and now in its 13th edition, aims at giving in simple form what a motor-cyclist needs to get the greatest pleasure, utmost reliability, longest life, speediest adjustments and the greatest efficiency from his engine. It does not, however, claim to deal exhaustively with *complete* dismantling or assembling because the expert technical mechanical ability of the reader may not be quite adequate, and because of the limited space at the author's disposal. In most instances of serious breakdown or failure one should consult a local Villiers mechanic or contact Norton–Villiers Ltd., Marston Road, Wolverhampton.

The more recent models covered in detail (with explanatory diagrams) are the Mark 6F (98 c.c.), 31C (148 c.c.), 2L (173 c.c.), 9E and 10E (197 c.c.), 31, 32, 32A, and 34A (246 c.c.), 2T (250 c.c. twin) and 3T (324 c.c. twin).

Earlier engines of which many are still in use and also dealt with fully are the Mark 4F (98 c.c.), 12D (122 c.c.), 29C and 30C (148 c.c.), 7E and 8E (197 c.c.). Earlier models are discussed only briefly in order to give a "picture" of the manner in which the modern engines have been developed. A copious index enables quick reference to be made to the particular item upon which help is needed.

I would express my grateful appreciation for the valuable help given me by Norton–Villiers Ltd., Marston Road, Wolverhampton, by way of technical details, diagrams and photographs.

CYRIL GRANGE

Contents

1	How the two-stroke engine works	1
2	Types of Villiers two-stroke motor-cycle engines	7
3	The Villiers flywheel magneto	18
4	The Villiers electric lighting systems	29
5	Villiers carburettors	42
6	Operating, handling and maintenance	56
7	Adjusting and overhauling	64
8	The Siba Dynastart	85
	Index	93

1 How the two-stroke engine works

THE two-stroke engine is the simplest, least complicated, cheapest and most reliable internal combustion engine, requiring as it does infrequent adjustment and overhaul and having a long life.

In order to obtain useful force, an explosive gas (in this case petrol vapour and air) has to be led into a fixed combustion chamber so that

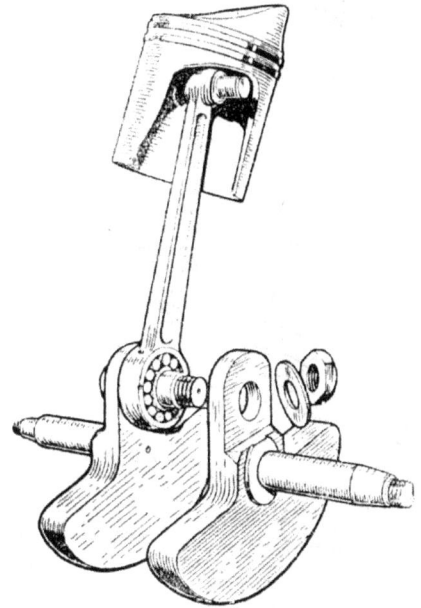

FIG. 1. THE MAIN MOVING COMPONENTS OF A TWO-STROKE ENGINE

when fired by heat (from a sparking plug) the expansion forces down a piston attached to a connecting rod which is, in turn, fitted to a crankshaft which is thus made to rotate and provide easily available power. In a two-stroke engine the gas is drawn from the carburettor into the crankcase via a passage (or port) in the cylinder wall which is opened (or uncovered) by the piston as it reaches the top of its stroke. This gas is transferred, when the piston reaches its lowest point, to the combustion head through

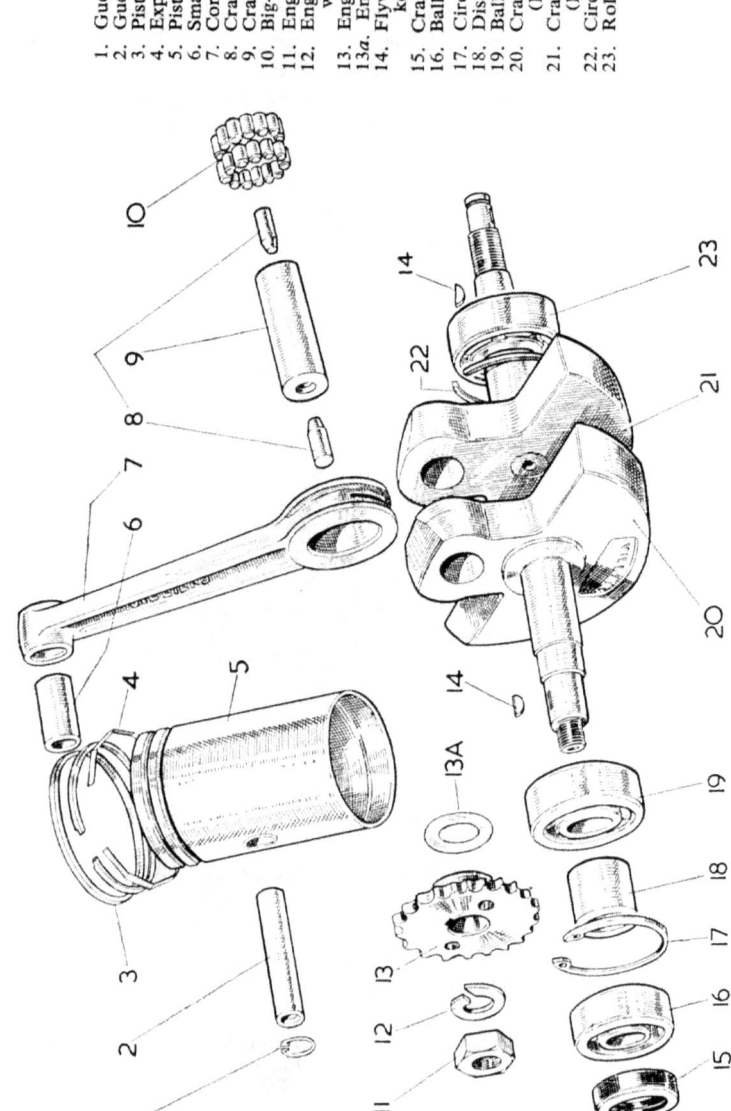

FIG. 2. PISTON AND CRANKSHAFT GROUP OF THE VILLIERS MARK 9E, 2L AND 31C ENGINES

1. Gudgeon-pin circlip
2. Gudgeon pin
3. Piston ring
4. Expander ring
5. Piston
6. Small-end bush
7. Connecting rod
8. Crank-pin plugs
9. Crank pin
10. Big-end rollers ¼ in. × ¼ in.
11. Engine-sprocket nut
12. Engine-sprocket-nut spring washer
13. Engine sprocket
13a. Engine-sprocket shim
14. Flywheel and engine-sprocket key
15. Crankcase oil-seal
16. Ball bearing
17. Circlip
18. Distance piece
19. Ball bearing
20. Crankweb and drive shaft (Mark 9E drive side)
21. Crankweb and drive shaft (Mark 9E magneto side)
22. Circlip
23. Roller race

a passage (or port), where it is ignited. The moving parts are, therefore, few and the engine is little affected by wear, heat or the forces of inertia.

The Working Components. There are only three major working components comprising the piston, connecting rod and crankshaft (Fig. 1). The PISTON, a cast-iron or aluminium alloy cylindrical body makes a gas-tight fit with the cylinder walls by being fitted with spring compression rings (piston rings) near its top, and moves up and down (reciprocates) in the cylinder bore. The piston is attached to a CONNECTING ROD by means of a gudgeon pin fitted through a bronze bush secured in the "small-end" of the connecting rod. The connecting rod is made of forged steel, its function being to transmit the downward thrust of the piston to the crankshaft thus changing the reciprocating motion of the piston into rotary movement of the crankshaft.

The CRANKSHAFT, which rotates in bearings fitted in each side of the crankcase, consists of a crank pin to which the lower part of the connecting rod is held by rollers (usually alternately bronze and steel) called the "big-end," and webs or balance weights.

The piston reciprocates in a cylinder in which the ports (or gas passages) are formed, a carburettor supplies the petrol-air mixture and a magneto the "spark"—the simplest possible arrangement. A piston and crankshaft group is shown in Fig. 2.

The Two-stroke Cycle of Operations. There are three designs, all of which work on the same principle but differ in the manner in which the gases are moved in (new charge) and out (burnt exhaust). The first design (Fig. 3) had three ports, one for inlet, one for transfer and one for exhaust and the new and burnt gases were kept apart in the combustion chamber, by the use of a piston which had a deflector head.

Engines of this type were in use from 1913 to 1934, and included the Mark I-V, VIc-XIIc, 1E-2E, VI A-XVI A, VI B-XIV B, and midgets for autocycles (1931).

The second design had seven ports, one for inlet, four for transfer and two for exhaust and it was now possible to use a flat-topped piston to make greater use of the explosive force. The incoming gas was now deflected by means of the redesigned transfer ports.

Flat-topped piston engines were the Mark 3C, 6E, XVII A-XVIII A, 8D and 9D.

For post-war engines, a third design (Fig. 4) was instituted in which there were four ports—one inlet, two transfer and one exhaust with the flat-topped piston feature retained. Greater efficiency resulted because of the use of a better balanced and less heavy piston, the more rapid expulsion of the exhaust gases and an improvement in thermal efficiency through the hemispherical cylinder head.

Engines of this type (1948 onwards) are the Mark 1F-2F (autocycle)

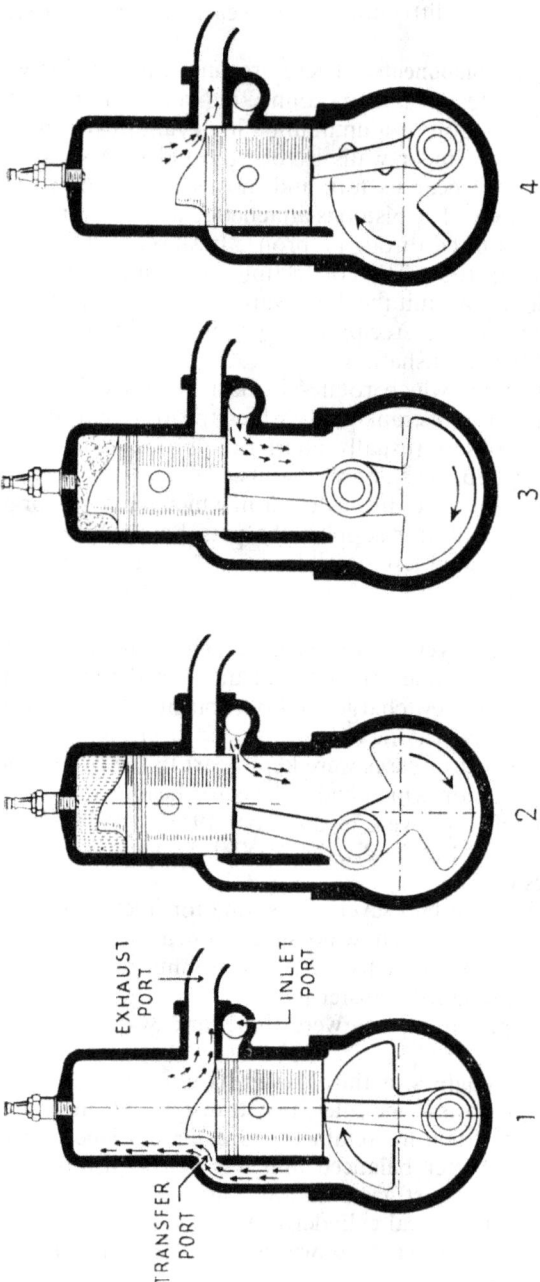

Fig. 3. Cycle of Operations of Three-port Two-stroke Engine

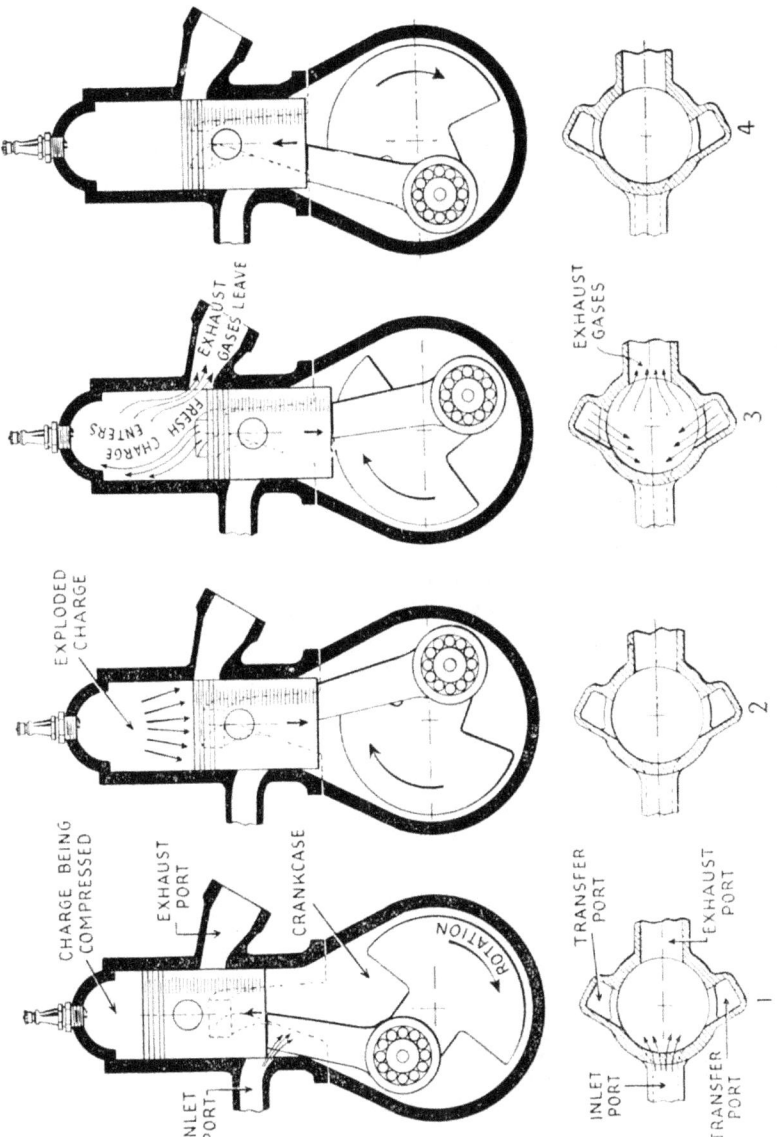

Fig. 4. Cycle of Operations of Four-port Two-stroke Engine

10D, 12D, 4F, 6F, 6E–10E, 2L, 1H, 2H, 2T, 3T, 4F, 6F, 31A, 9E, and 29C–31C.

How It Works. Only by knowing what happens inside the engine can one get the best out of it, effect rapid diagnosis of trouble and apply the appropriate remedy. Let us follow the operation from Fig. 4 which shows the design of current models. In (1) the piston is moving upwards and as it compresses the mixture of petrol and air it also creates suction in the crankcase so that as the inlet port (to which the carburettor is attached) is opened by the rising piston, a new charge rushes into the crankcase.

Just before the piston reaches its top position, the spark fires the charge and the piston is forced down (2) on its power stroke first closing the inlet port and then opening the exhaust port and at the same time compressing the new charge in the crankcase. The burnt gases escape (3) and a new charge quickly comes up into the cylinder from the crankcase via the two transfer ports. The piston then moves upward (4) closing inlet, exhaust and transfer ports and compresses the charge to continue the cycle as in (1).

The explosive charge is, therefore, fired in the cylinder-head space each two strokes of the piston, so providing a power surge with each revolution of the crankshaft; hence the smooth running.

With the earlier three-port design, the piston had a special shaped head, the purpose of which was to deflect the charge upwards from the one transfer port into the cylinder head space. (*See* Fig. 3.)

2 Types of Villiers two-stroke motor-cycle engines

VILLIERS engines may be single cylinder with separate gearbox, single cylinder with integral gearbox or twin-cylinder engine-gear units. It is important to be able to identify the particular engine so that the right spares can be obtained. Each unit is distinguished by its name or mark number cast on the outside of the transfer port on the cylinder and every engine has a number, with one or more prefix letters, stamped on the sprocket side of the crankcase immediately below the cylinder flange, or on one of the top crankcase lugs just below the cylinder base. When ordering spares, the engine type, number and prefix letters must be given along with the part number and description.

The capacity of an engine is the volume of the cylinder swept by the piston, usually measured in cubic centimetres (c.c.) and for rough comparison 100 c.c. is taken as representing one horse-power (h.p.) although the actual output is usually much more. For instance, the Mark 4F engine of 98 c.c. (6 cu in.) develops 2·8 b.h.p. at 4,000 r.p.m. (revolutions per minute). Note: horse-power (h.p.) is only a nominal rating and bears little relation to the actual power output of an engine which is expressed in brake horse-power (b.h.p.).

The range of types covers all possible needs and many well-known motor-cycle manufacturers have fitted Villiers engines as standard with extreme satisfaction ever since the first engine, known as the Mark 1, which was made in 1913.

It will be helpful to have a list of the main types. Of those of pre-war manufacture brief details are given, but of the current models full specifications.

98 c.c. Engines. The first "Midget" model (1931) prefix letters CY, used in lightweight machines, had a bore and stroke of 50 mm, cast iron deflector piston, and roller-bearing big end, but was of a special three-port design in that the exhaust and transfer ports were arranged on the side of the cylinder in line with the crankshaft.

The "Junior" followed with a similar specification, except that it was built with a reduction gear and clutch as one unit.

The modern counterpart is the "Junior" de-luxe (Fig. 5, page 8) with the same bore and stroke. The design is, however, different, the piston has a flat top, the cylinder four transfer and two exhaust ports, and the

Fig. 5. The 98 c.c. "Junior" De-luxe Engine

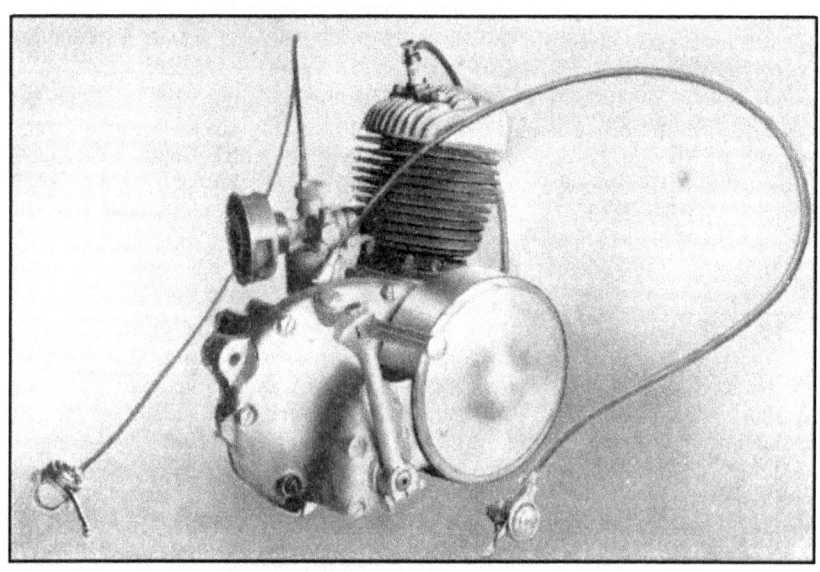

Fig. 6. The 98 c.c. Mark 1F Engine and Gearbox Unit

detachable cylinder head is made of light alloy. A three-pole flywheel magneto with lighting set is fitted and the carburettor is the "Junior" type (pages 43-4).

THE MARK 1F (Fig. 6). This has proved a popular two-speed engine-gear unit with a bore of 47 mm and a stroke of 57 mm. The maximum b.h.p. is 2·8 at 4,000 r.p.m., and gear ratios are 1·54 to 1 and 1 to 1. Starting is by kick-starter with folding pedal and the gears are operated by a sliding dog clutch from the handle-bar control lever. The weight is only 38 lb and an average petrol consumption figure is 140 m.p.g.

The cast-iron cylinder is deeply finned and has two transfer ports and one exhaust port topped by a detachable aluminium-alloy head. The flat-topped light alloy piston carries a floating gudgeon pin located endways by circlips. The "big-end" is made up of two rows of steel rollers, the crankshaft, with double crankwebs, being carried by a large ball journal-bearing on each side.

The Villiers flywheel magneto provides high-tension current for ignition, and for lighting the alternating current being rectified by a Westinghouse rectifier for charging a 6 volt 10 amp-hour battery. The carburettor is a Villiers "Junior" Type 6/0 (page 44).

MARK 2F. This engine superseded the "Junior" de-luxe (10 years in production) and the unit follows the same specification as the Mark 1F except that it has no gear unit. It has a compression release valve and uses a "Junior" carburettor but without the oil-wetted gauze air filter. It develops a maximum of 2 b.h.p. at 3,750 r.p.m. and the gear ratio of engine to clutch (two-plate cork insert type) is 2·47 to 1.

A flywheel magneto provides current for both ignition and lighting, the latter with specially increased output (6 volt 12 watt). The weight is 31 lb and petrol consumption at the rate of 120 m.p.g.

MARK 4F. This two-speed engine-gear unit follows the design of the well-tried Mark 1F, with which it is interchangeable. Actually, there is little difference except that a rubber oil-seal replaces the spring-loaded gland between the engine sprocket and crankcase and that the magneto is now completely enclosed and rubber sealed so that no oil from the gearbox can reach the magneto or the crankcase.

From 1953 the gearbox ratios were changed to 1·64 to 1 and 1 to 1 and gear control is from the handlebar by Bowden cable.

Recent models have the Type S.12 carburettor in place of the "Junior" type instrument.

The six-pole magneto provides current both for ignition and lighting but for the latter there is a choice of two types of equipment—

(*a*) direct current to the lamps via the headlamp switch, near which is a small dry battery (Ever-Ready 800) for the parking lights, and

(*b*) a selenium-type rectifier converts the alternating current to a direct current for charging a 6 volt, 10 amp-hour battery.

MARK 6F (Fig. 7). This two-speed unit having a capacity of 98 c.c. is similar to the Mark 4F except that the gears are changed by the foot which has necessitated modifying the clutch and gear casing. The Mark 6F/H takes the same modified casing but gear control is by cable from the handlebar.

122 c.c. Engines. MARK 9D: this unit is a compact assembly of engine, three-speed gearbox, clutch and kick-starter. The engine which has a

FIG. 7. THE 98 C.C. MARK 6F ENGINE

bore of 50 mm and a stroke of 62 mm has a flat-top piston, ball and roller bearings throughout, two exhaust ports, four transfer ports and one inlet port.

Three types of carburettor have been fitted to this model i.e. Midget, Lightweight having single-lever control and external adjustment to taper needle for starting and Lightweight, having internal adjustment and a separate strangler.

On the early versions, two-pole magnetos were used but later 18 or 24 watt six-pole instruments were fitted. The weight is under 40 lb, the fuel consumption is at the rate of 110 m.p.g. and the maximum output is 4 b.h.p.

MARK 10D. The engine and three-speed gearbox are bolted together to make one assembly. The four-port engine has a bore of 50 mm and a stroke of 62 mm, the maximum b.h.p. at 4,400 r.p.m. being 4·8. The earlier gearbox ratios were 3·25, 1·7 and 1 to 1, but closer ratios were later introduced (indicated by suffix letter D after the engine number) of 2·66, 1·4 and 1 to 1. Conversion from wide to narrow ratios is easily carried out by fitting a high-gear pinion of 24 teeth and a layshaft fixed pinion of

TYPES OF VILLIERS MOTOR-CYCLE ENGINES

18 teeth. The carburettor is the single-lever Type 3/4, and the magneto a six-pole unit providing for direct lighting or via a 6-volt battery charged through a rectifier. From 1951 an a.c./d.c. lighting set was introduced with a four-position switch.

THE MARK 12D (Fig. 8) engine and three-speed unit (kick-starter), replaces the Mark 10D with which it can be interchanged. It is identified by the motif on the crankcase cover and the oil-filter plug at the top. Crankcase compression is held by rubber oil-seals. The connecting rod

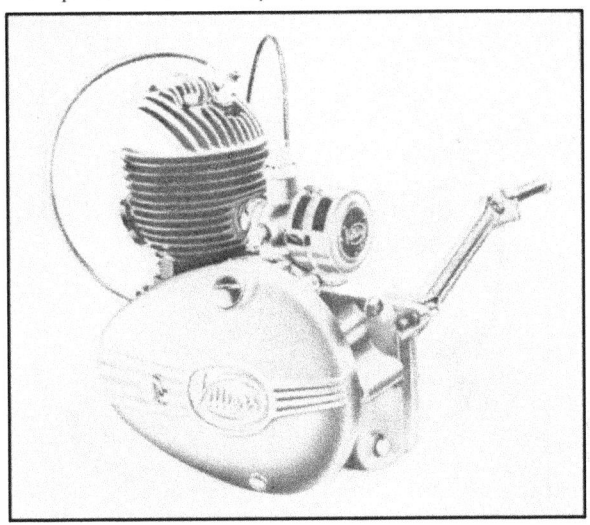

FIG. 8. 122 C.C. MARK 12D ENGINE AND THREE-SPEED GEARBOX UNIT

big-end bearings now consist of 12 steel $\frac{1}{4}$ in. × $\frac{1}{4}$ in. rollers with six bronze spacing rollers. An innovation (for Villiers) is the fitting of a gasket between the cylinder top and head.

The gearbox ratios are 2·55, 1·34 and 1 to 1, the carburettor is a Type S.19 and the magneto is a six-pole type providing for a direct or a rectifier lighting set (page 29).

The competition version, the Mark 11D, can be fitted with gears of a special ratio for scrambles and speed trials. With a compression ratio of 10 to 1 it develops 6 b.h.p. at 4,600 r.p.m.

147–148 c.c. Engines. The year 1922 saw the introduction of the range of 147 c.c. engines with the Mark VI–C. They had cast-iron pistons, fixed gudgeon pins and a one-piece cylinder with compression release valve mounted in the top. The Mark VIII–C with a floating padded gudgeon pin, and later with an inertia ring, proved outstanding and was in production up to 1947.

The popular Mark 29C and Mark 30C were the first 147 c.c. engine-gearbox units, in which the engine had the flat-topped piston and one exhaust, one inlet and two transfer ports. Both in design and construction, these 147 c.c. unit-construction power units closely resemble the Mark 11D and Mark 12D.

Both have a bore of 55 mm and a stroke of 62 mm giving a capacity of 147 c.c. or 9 cu in. The Mark 29C has a four-speed gearbox with ratios of 3·47, 2·3, 1·35 and 1 to 1 and similar in design to the gearboxes used on Mark 11D/4, 8E/4 and 7E/4 a carburettor Type S.25, and a special

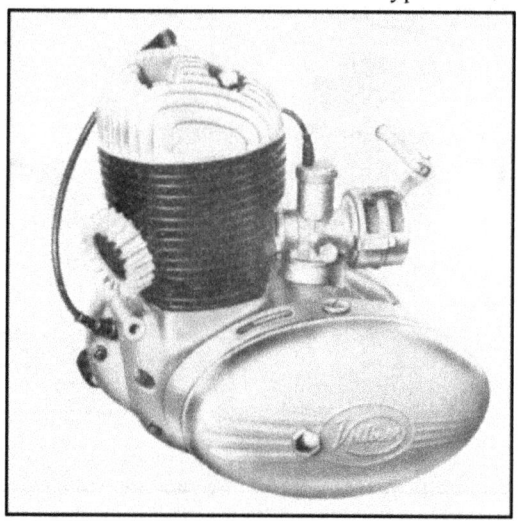

FIG. 9. 148 C.C. MARK 31C ENGINE AND GEARBOX UNIT

magneto with ignition coil and long-dwell-cam flywheel. The maximum b.h.p. at 4,500 r.p.m. is 6.

THE MODEL 30C three-speed gearbox has ratios of 2·55, 1·34 and 1 to 1, and is similar to that used with Mark 12D and Mark 8E/3 engine-gear units. The carburettor is the Type S.19. The lighting-rectifier sets are similar to those used on the Mark 4F, 6F and 6F/4 units (page 30). At 4,300 r.p.m., 5·4 b.h.p. is produced.

The engine and gearbox unit designated to the Mark 31C (Fig. 9) not in current production is a well-proved successor to the Mark 30C. The bore is 57 mm and the stroke 58 mm giving a capacity of 148 c.c. or 9·03 cu in. The carburettor is the Type S.19 with oil-wetted filter and air strangler. Ignition is by a totally enclosed flywheel magneto giving either 6 or 12 volts direct or rectifier lighting (page 24).

In this range are the following: the Mark 31C/3 with three-speed gearbox; Mark 31C/4 with four-speed gearbox; Mark 31C/3KF has a three-speed gearbox and the Mark 31C/4KF a four-speed gearbox, both units have a kick-starter and blower cooling; and Mark 31C/3SF with three-speed box or the Mark 31C/4SF with four-speed box, both with self-starter and blower cooling.

The standard three-speed ratios are 2·55, 1·34 and 1 to 1; wide, 3·25, 1·7 and 1 to 1. The four-speed ratios are, standard, 2·94, 1·78, 1·27 and 1 to 1 and wide, 3·6, 2·4, 1·34 and 1 to 1.

The engine has the modern cast-iron cylinder, detachable aluminium-alloy head, four ports and a flat-topped alloy two-ring piston. The maximum b.h.p. at 5,000 r.p.m. is 6·6.

173 c.c. Engines. In the early thirties, four models were made under "sports" designations but the only engine and gearbox unit in long-term production is the Mark 2L and is interchangeable with the Mark 9E unit and Mark 31C unit. A bore of 59 mm and stroke of 63·5 mm gives it a capacity of 173 c.c. (10·55 cu in.). It uses carburettor Type S.22 and has the same gearbox ratios as the Mark 31C. At 5,000 r.p.m. the maximum b.h.p. is 7·4. The range consists of Marks 2L/3, 2L/4, 2L/3KF, or 4KF and 2L/3SF or 4SF. The weight is 67 lb, and fuel consumption is at the rate of 110 m.p.g.

197 c.c. Engines. Right from the Mark 1E in 1928, the super sports in 1929 and the 3E in 1938 to the recent Marks 6E, 7E, 8E and 9E, this 200 c.c. class model has been most popular.

THE MARK 6E engine-gear unit (Fig. 10) has a bore of 59 mm and stroke of 72 mm the capacity being 197 c.c., or 12·02 cu in. It develops 8·4 b.h.p. at 4,000 r.p.m. The design is similar to that of the Mark 10D and is interchangeable with the frame lugs. The three gearbox ratios are 2·66, 1·4 and 1 to 1. The carburettor is the two-lever Type 4/5.

THE MARK 8E (produced up to early 1959) has a similar specification to, and replaces and is interchangeable with the Mark 6E, the gear ratios being 2·55, 1·34 and 1 to 1. By replacing the normal layshaft and high-gear pinions with gears having 26 and 16 teeth, ratios of 3·25 and 1·7 respectively become available. The four-speed gearbox ratios are 2·93, 1·8, 1·35 and 1 to 1, but a wide ratio box is available. The carburettor is the Type S.24 and the magneto a six-pole direct or rectifier unit.

THE MARK 7E is the high-compression (8·25 to 10 to 1) unit for competition work with a three- or four-speed gearbox and producing 9·3 b.h.p. at 4,300 r.p.m.

The 197 c.c. engine-gear unit whose production started in 1955 is THE MARK 9E (Fig. 51) with three- or four-speed gearbox, with or without Siba Dynastart and blower cooling and with a standard compression ratio of 7·25 to 1. On trials or sports machines the compression ratio is 8·25 to 1. With standard cylinder head the engine develops 8 b.h.p. at 4,000 r.p.m. The Mark 9E/4SFR has a forward or reverse running engine.

The three- or four-speed gearbox ratios are the same as those for the

Mark 31C. The unit is designed to provide a 10 degree forward inclination of the cylinder. The weight is 67 lb and fuel consumption at the rate of approximately 85 m.p.g. The carburettor is the Type S.25.

THE MARK 10E is identical with the Mark 9E except that certain

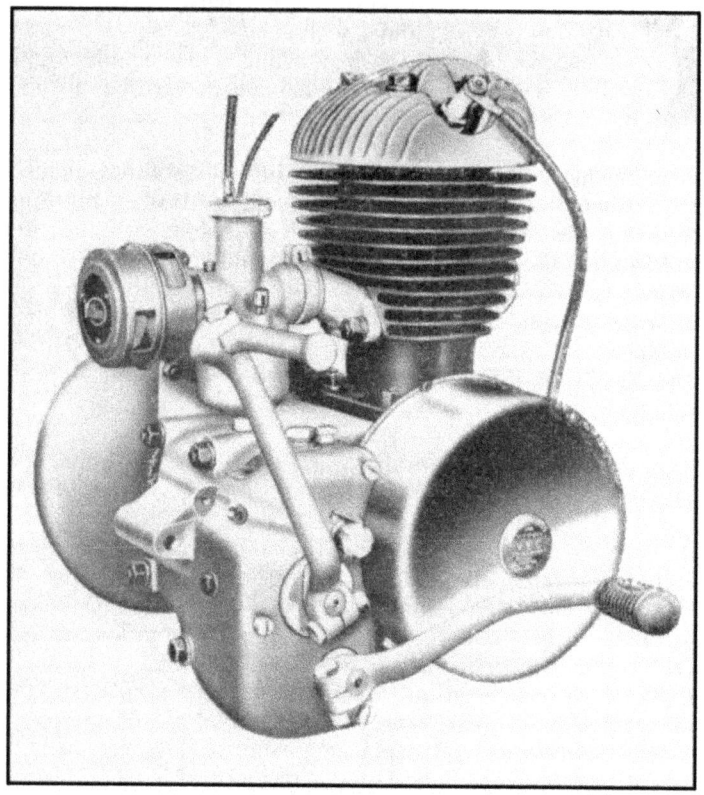

FIG. 10. THE 197 C.C. MARK 6E ENGINE-GEAR UNIT

modifications allow it to be used when the machine design necessitates the engine being vertical in the frame.

225 c.c. Engines. The Mark 1H is an interesting engine-gear unit (first manufactured in 1953 and in use for many years) in that the gearbox and crankcase were so compact and streamlined that the unit appeared as one component, although the two parts were, in effect, bolted together. The bore of 63 mm and stroke of 72 mm, gives a capacity of 225 c.c. or 13·73 cu in. and a maximum power output at 4,500 r.p.m. of 9·6 b.h.p. The carburettor is the Type S.25.

TYPES OF VILLIERS MOTOR-CYCLE ENGINES   15

246 c.c. Engines. The larger version of the Mark 1H was the Mark 2H with 66 mm bore and 72 mm stroke giving a capacity of 246 c.c. or 15 cu in. and an output, with a compression ratio of 7·25 to 1, of 11 b.h.p. at 4,500 r.p.m.

The latest unit is the Mark 31A with the same bore and stroke. It has a three- or four-speed gearbox with ratios as for the Mark 2L and is with or without self-starter and reverse. The design is as the Mark 31C (*see* Fig. 9).

250 c.c. Engines. The Mark 2T Villiers engine shown in Fig. 11 is

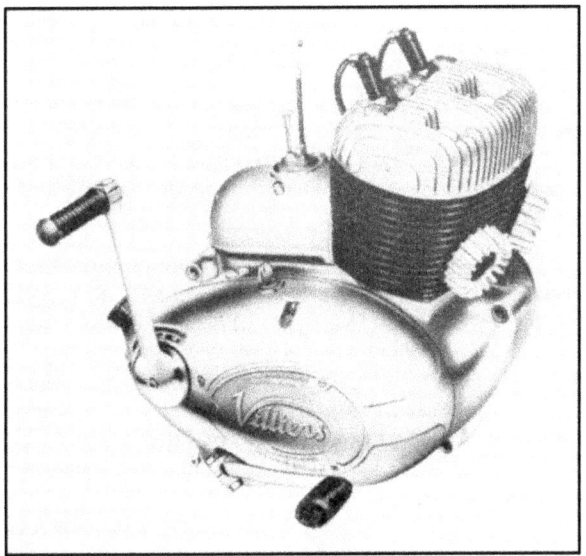

FIG. 11. THE 250 C.C. MARK 2T TWIN-CYLINDER ENGINE AND GEAR UNIT

the first side-by-side twin built as a unit with the gearbox. It consists in effect of two single-cylinder engines assembled side by side with crankshafts coupled to give 180-degree firing intervals. The centre main roller bearing and oil-seal are housed in a circular centre-plate, whilst a ball bearing and a roller bearing support the built-up crankshaft on the drive side and generator side respectively. The lubrication of the main bearings is supplemented by oil drain holes in the crankcase. Roller-bearing big-ends are employed. The small-ends have steel-backed bronze bushes. The solid-skirt, flat-topped pistons each have two rings, the lower ones having expanders fitted behind them and, following Villiers practice, the gudgeon-pin bosses are bronze-bushed. The separate light-alloy cylinder heads have half-pear-shaped combustion chambers, and the compression ratio is 8·2 to 1. Bore and stroke measurements for this engine, which produces 15 b.h.p. at 5,500 r.p.m. are 50 mm and 63·5 mm respectively. Ignition arrangements include twin contact-breakers and H.T. coils in conjunction with the flywheel generator which also provides lighting current. A Villiers Type S.22/2 carburettor is fitted, and the complete unit weighs 94 lb.

The standard gearbox ratios are 3·06, 1·9, 1·325 and 1 to 1 and the wide ratios 3·6, 2·02, 1·4 and 1 to 1. A separate self-energizing ignition system is used to each cylinder.

The Mark 2T/SFR and SR engines can be started either in a forward or reverse direction but it is important that the first-gear position only is used when the engine is running in reverse.

324 c.c. Engines. The Mark 3T was developed from the Mark 2T by using a larger cylinder bore of 57 mm and a stroke of 63·5 mm giving a capacity of 324 c.c. or 19·7 cu in. and an output at 5,000 r.p.m. of 16 b.h.p. with a compression ratio of 7·25 to 1. Gearbox ratios and carburettor are as for the Mark 2T.

For Trials Work and Racing. There are four engines used for racing, trials and scrambles. Marks 9E/4 and 32A are to be recommended for trials and sports work and Marks 33A/4 and 34A/4 for racing and scrambling. The Mark 9E/4 is of 197 c.c. capacity with a competition compression ratio of 8·25 to 1 and four-speed gearbox. The carburettor is the Type S.25 model with No. 3 throttle and No. $3\frac{1}{2}$ needle jets. The plug commonly used is the Lodge HH14 (or other comparable type) with a gap of 0·018 to 0·025 in. The spark is timed $\frac{11}{64}$ in. plus or minus $\frac{1}{64}$ in. before top-dead-centre.

Lubrication is as indicated in the chart on page 62. Particulars of this engine are to be found on pages 74–5.

MARK 32A/4. This engine is of 246 c.c. capacity with a compression ratio of 7·9 to 1. The four-speed gearbox provides ratios of 2·9, 1·78, 1·27 and 1 to 1. The throttle jet is No. 4. Other specification details are as for the Mark 9E/4.

THE MARK 33A/4. Of 246 c.c. capacity, this has a specially high compression-ratio of 12 to 1 and a four-speed gearbox with ratios of 2·55, 1·78, 1·27 and 1 to 1. The carburettor generally used is the Amal 289 with 109 needle jet, 370 c.c. main jet, 25 pilot jet and throttle No. $3\frac{1}{2}$ (Amal) and taper needle D (in No. 3 groove). The sparking plug is a Lodge R147 or RL49 with 0·018 to 0·022 in. gap and spark timing of $\frac{1}{8}$ in. to $\frac{5}{32}$ in. before top-dead-centre. The petrol-oil mixture is one part Castrol R to 24 parts petrol. Other details are as for the Mark 9E/4.

Electric Starter. Electric starters are available on the following engines: The Mark 31C/3SF or 4SF (148 c.c.); Mark 2L/3SF or 4SF (173 c.c.);

TYPES OF VILLIERS MOTOR-CYCLE ENGINES   17

Mark 9E/3S or 4S, Mark 9E/3SR or 4SR, Mark 9E/4SF or 4SFR (197 c.c.); Mark 31A/4S or 4SR (246 c.c.). The last-named also have a kick-starter.

Blower Cooling. Engines provided with a blower fan and cowling are the Mark 31C/3KF or 4KF and Mark 31C/3SF or 4SF (148 c.c.); Mark 2L/3KF or 4KF and Mark 2L/3SF or 4SF (173 c.c.); Mark 9E/4SF or 4SFR (197 c.c.).

In the foregoing Mark designations, 3 and 4 indicate number of gearbox speeds, K, kick-starter, F, blower cooling, R, reverse gear and S, electric starter.

The components of the latest type cowled engine with electric starter are shown in Chapter 7, Fig. 54, page 80.

Engines for Invalid Carriages. The engines used for powering invalid carriages were the Mark 8E and the Mark 9E and these gave excellent results. They have now been replaced by the Mark 11E, which is basically similar to the Mark 9E, except that the crankcase is reshaped and lightened and there have been minor changes made in the chaincase, fan casing, top cowl, gearbox and end cover. There are now two instead of nine co-axial circumferential clutch springs. There is also a new type clutch push-rod at the lever end, bridge and thrust bearing for lever.

The engines used for powering invalid carriages are fitted with the Siba Dynastart equipment, fan and cowling.

Three- and Four-wheeled Light Cars. The Mark 6E, Mark 8E, Mark 9E and Mark 31A, have all been used to power the Bond Minicar whilst the blower-cooled Mark 9E is fitted to the Hunslett Scootacar and the Frisky three-wheeler.

The Mark 3T has been used to drive the Friskysport four-wheeled car and is also used to power the de-luxe version of the Hunslett Scootacar. For these applications the engine is equipped with the Siba Dynastart and turbo-blower cooling. The Mark 9E is used in Go-kart racing.

Boat Propulsion. The Mark 2T and 3T have been used by amateurs and for experimental purposes for boat propulsion, but so far nothing serious in the way of production has resulted.

Lawn Mowers. None of the engines dealt with in this book is used for lawn mowers, for which application Villiers make special industrial units.

3 The Villiers flywheel magneto

How It Works. If a conductor or core of soft iron is wound with heavy-gauge insulated copper wire (called a "primary" coil) and then insulated wire of a finer gauge is wound round over this (called the "secondary" coil) the heart or *"armature"* of the magneto is built up. (*See A* Fig. 12.)

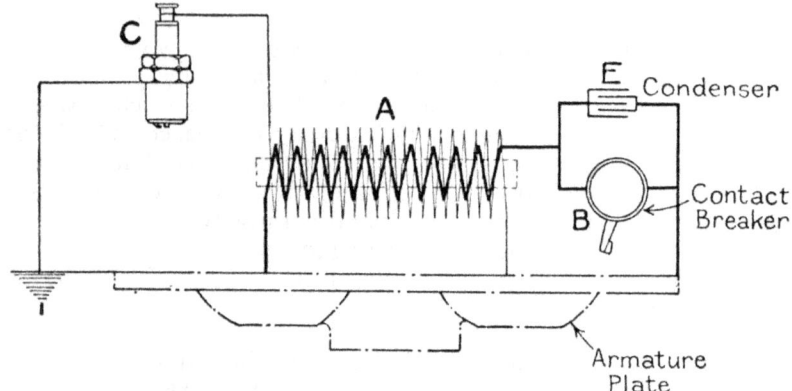

FIG. 12. DIAGRAM OF THE ELECTRICAL CIRCUIT IN A MAGNETO

By rotating the flywheel, inside the edge of which are magnets, a low-tension electric current is induced in the primary coil. If this current is broken by a "contact-breaker" (*B*), a high pressure current (H.T.) is set up in the secondary coil. It is this current which, in its efforts to return to "earth," produces a spark across the points of a sparking plug (*C*) which is placed in the circuit. The current then travels to "earth" via the body of the sparking plug.

The condenser (*E*) is connected in parallel with the contact-breaker points, its purpose being to stop sparking at the points at the moment of the break and to store up the current in the primary winding until the spark is required. The condenser must therefore be in perfect order.

You should know the practical application of the contact-breaker the purpose of which is to break the circuit in the primary winding and cause a spark to jump the plug points. The "works" are in a small circular metal box usually fitted with a cover. At the back is the condenser and on view are the stationary contact point and the point on the moving rocker-arm the end of which contacts the cam on the flywheel boss and thus opens or closes the points.

Adjusting the Contact-breaker. Although attention to the contact-breaker is rarely needed, it is important that the contacts should be kept clean and properly adjusted. The flywheel should be rotated clockwise so that the rocker arm is lifted to its highest position by the operating cam so that the points are fully open. Screw A (Figs. 13 and 14), which is a

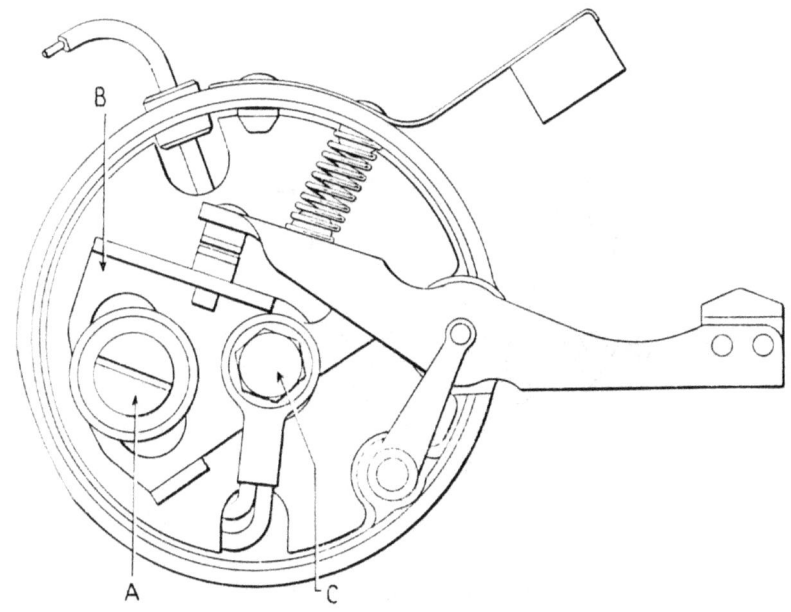

FIG. 13. ADJUSTING THE CONTACT-BREAKER POINTS

lock-nut, should be slightly loosened and the baseplate B moved with a screwdriver so that the points are 0·015 in. ($\frac{1}{64}$ in.) apart. A feeler gauge should, of course, be used. Screw A is now tightened, the gauge withdrawn and the points rechecked. Screw C (Fig. 13) or screw D (Fig. 14) is not touched as it carried the lead from the ignition coil and condenser. On some engines, e.g. Marks 29C and 30C, there is an adjusting cam C (Fig. 14) which, when turned, closes or opens the points. It is not necessary to remove the flywheel to get at the points as the contact-breaker can be reached through the flywheel "spokes."

If you think that poor or difficult starting is due to the magneto, hold the high-tension lead $\frac{1}{8}$ in. from the cylinder, rotate the flywheel and, if the spark is very weak, check up on the following: contact-breaker points may be too close together, oiled up, badly pitted or dirty; high-tension lead making poor contact with ignition coil (not with Marks 1H, 2H, and 3T, engines); poor connexion to low-tension wire; moisture on condenser; damaged insulation on fixed contact. If there is no spark the cause may be any of the foregoing or a faulty ignition coil or condenser (the latter more likely).

THE CONTACT POINTS. These must be kept clean or there may be erratic running or difficult starting. They should be wiped occasionally with a clean rag or with a small soft brush, soaked in petrol. The contact points

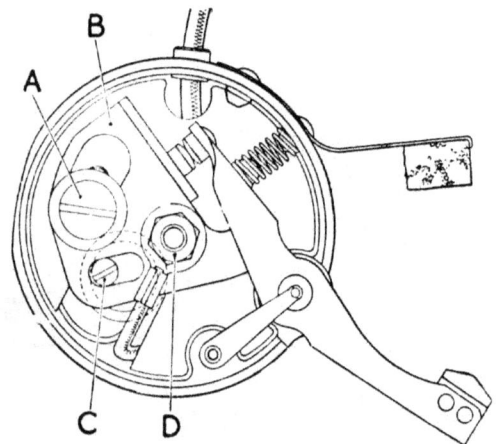

FIG. 14. CONTACT-BREAKER ASSEMBLY (MARKS 29C AND 30C)

should be clean, and make square contact. Should the contacts be badly burnt, which can happen after a long period of use, replacements may be necessary. If they are only slightly pitted your local garage will correct this. In some engines—the Mark 2F, for example, a felt pad impregnated with grease, keeps the cam lubricated. Should the pad be found to be dry it can be given a limited quantity of heavy oil or better still removed and soaked in molten high-temperature grease. Care should be taken to prevent oil or grease reaching the contact points.

In addition to the foregoing you should inspect the high-tension lead to the plug to see that it has not pulled away from the magneto frame or burnt through on a hot cylinder. Check the carbon brush on the ignition coil to see that it is held properly or that the armature plate screws have not become loose. The troubles which you may well get are not always to be found in the maker's handbook.

When attending to the contact-breaker assembly, be sure to replace all the fibre washers and to renew any that are faulty.

THE VILLIERS FLYWHEEL MAGNETO

Similar faults may occur with the assembly of the Mark 4F and 6F engines where a phosphor-bronze U-shaped contact strip is fitted at one end to the hexagon nut and with the other end under the arm of the rocker-arm spring (Fig. 15). It is important that there is no metallic contact between the point bracket and the contact strip and the two condenser leads.

Flywheel Removal. Should it be found necessary to remove the flywheel ou will require a special Villiers Hammer-tight spanner to loosen the

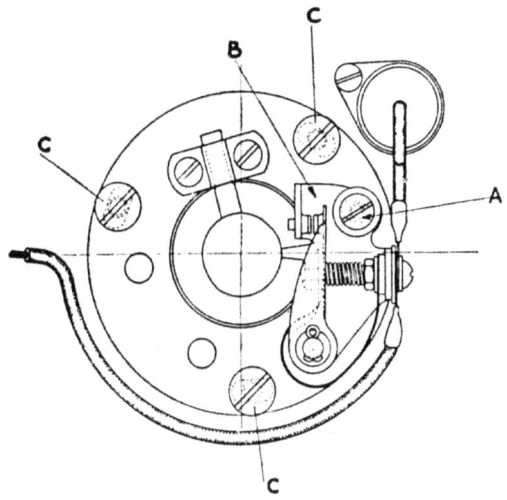

FIG. 15. CONTACT-BREAKER ASSEMBLY (MARKS 4F AND 6F)

centre nut which has a right-hand thread. After one or two turns the nut will be felt to tighten and if rotation is continued the extracting flange will pull out the flywheel. It will be necessary to use a hammer on the special spanner until the flywheel loosens on its shaft. When ordering the spanner it is necessary to give the model and number of the engine.

With the six-pole-type flywheel magneto the ignition and lighting coils and the contact-breaker are fitted to the armature plate which is held to the crankcase by four or six screws. You can take off the high-tension lead from the ignition coil to the sparking plug by unscrewing it from the armature plate, but it is most important when refitting it to be sure that the brass pad held by the spring and secured to the terminal makes good contact with the disc which is soldered on the outside of the ignition coil.

The shoes and magnets are usually screwed into the flywheel which is balanced and magnetized after the final machining. No purpose is served by removing these magnets; if you feel that the magnets may have lost some of their magnetism, which is unlikely, then the best plan is to remove the flywheel and send it to the manufacturers for servicing.

Flywheel Refitting. The flywheel must be fitted on to the shaft in proper relation to the position of the piston so that ignition takes place when the piston is, usually, $\frac{1}{8}$ in. to $\frac{1}{4}$ in. before top-dead-centre.

In early type engines, timing marks were stamped on the rim of the flywheel and on the end of the driving shaft, and when these were in line the timing was correct.

On later models, the timing marks are to be found on the flywheel rim and on the armature plate. These give rather more accurate timing.

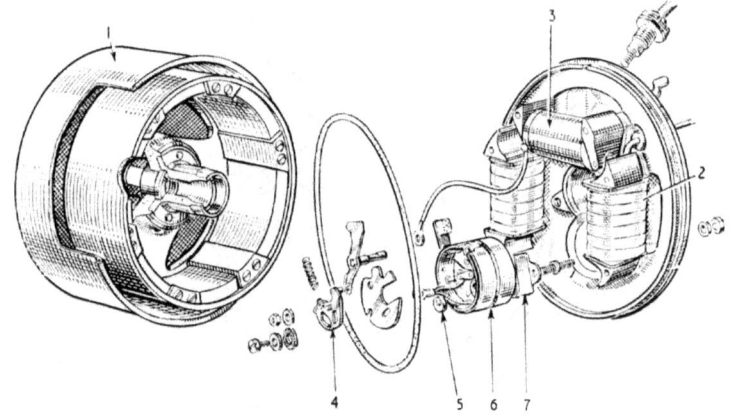

FIG. 16. MAGNETO (MARKS 29C AND 30C)

1. Flywheel assembly
2. Lighting coils
3. High-tension coil
4. Point bracket
5. Point bracket adjuster cam
6. Condenser box
7. Condenser

The way to time the engine is to rotate the crankshaft in a clockwise direction from the magneto side until the piston is the right distance before top-dead-centre (*see* page 27). The flywheel is then put on loosely and rotated without turning the crankshaft until the points just start to open. Then tighten up the flywheel nut just sufficient to hold it on to crankshaft, rotate again to check that the piston is at the top-dead-centre and the timing marks should coincide. The centre nut can then be carefully tightened up with the Hammer-tight spanner and the flywheel cover put on.

It is important that the contact-breaker points be set to the gap of 0·015 in. before the magneto is timed.

To Check Timing. Should it be felt that the timing could be improved, the cover should be removed so that the contact-breaker mechanism can be seen and the sparking plug taken out so that the piston top can be seen

THE VILLIERS FLYWHEEL MAGNETO

or felt. The shaft should be rotated until the points are just starting to open and at this point the piston should be $\frac{1}{8}$ in. to $\frac{1}{4}$ in. before top-dead-centre.

If there does seem to be any inaccuracy, remove the flywheel and adjust as already described.

Similar instructions to the foregoing also apply to the Marks 29C and 30C but to assist dismantling, Fig. 16 gives details.

In order to give the greatest possible assistance to owner-driver-mechanics, details are now given affecting specific types of engine in current use.

In the case of the Marks 4F and 6F, the timing can be corrected by moving the plate which carries the contact-breaker assembly clockwise to

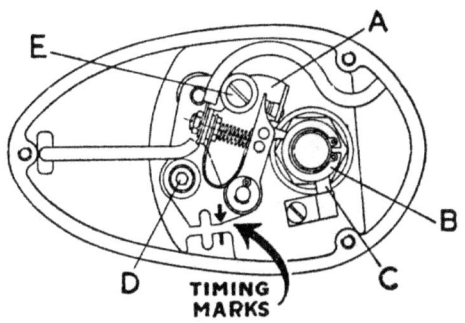

FIG. 17. TIMING IGNITION (MARKS 31A, 32A, 34A, 31C, 9E, 10E, 2L)

advance the ignition, and anti-clockwise to retard it. The plate is loosened from the crankcase by slackening the screws marked C (see Fig. 15). They should be securely tightened up after the correct adjustment has been obtained.

With Marks 31A, 32A, 34A, 9E, 10E, 2L, and 31C, if you need to retime the ignition, the solder filling the screw head at D, Fig. 17 must be removed, the screw loosened and the base plate moved to the left to advance or to the right to retard the ignition timing. The gap of the contact-breaker can be reset after releasing screw E.

Both adjustments will have to be repeated until the piston position and the point gap are correct after which screws D and E must be carefully tightened.

The contact-breaker assembly, Marks 31A, 32A, 34A, 31C, 9E, 10E, 2L, is shown in Fig. 18 and armature plate, flywheel in Fig. 19. To adjust the ignition timing after dismantling refer to Fig. 17. First, set the contact-breaker gap. The base plate of the contact-breaker should be set so that the two tuning marks are in line with one another. Move the piston to top-dead-centre and adjust the bracket which carries point A to provide a contact-breaker point gap of 0·012 in. to 0·015 in. Tighten the locking screw E.

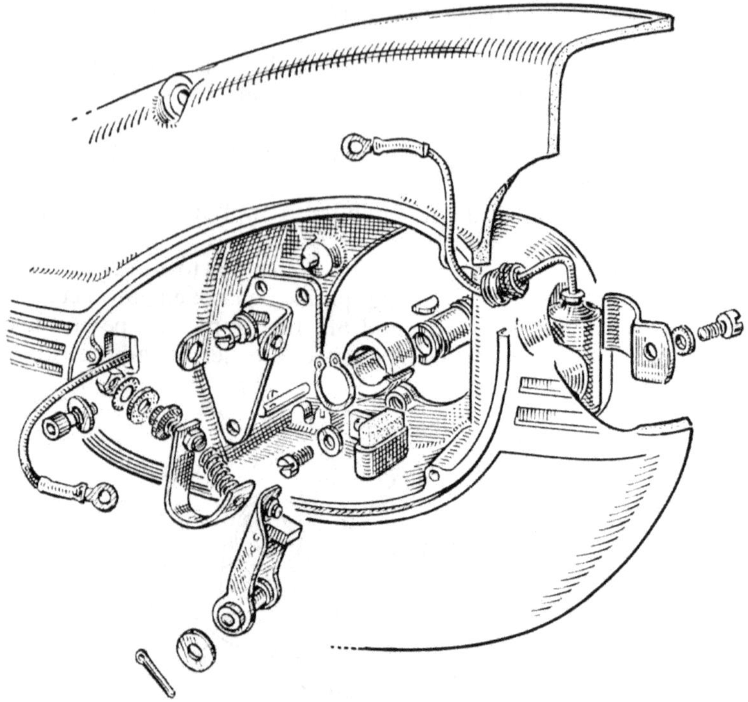

Fig. 18. Contact-breaker Assembly (Marks 31A, 32A, 34A, 31C, 9E, 10E, 2L)

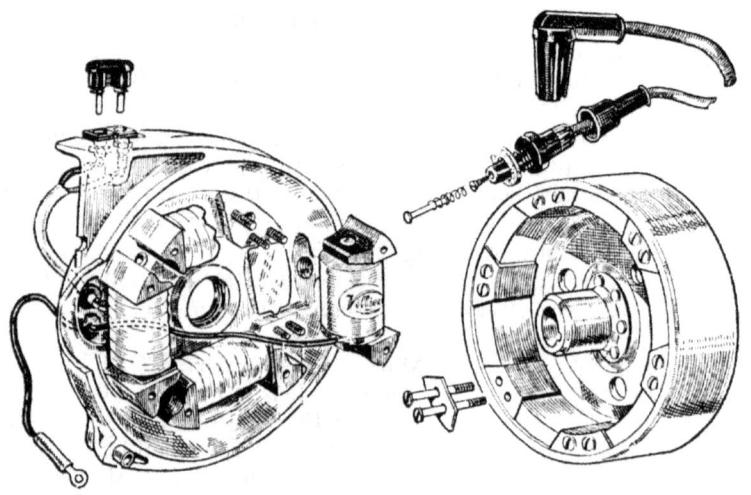

Fig. 19. Armature Plate and Flywheel Group of the 6-volt Ignition and Lighting Unit (Marks 31A, 31C, 9E, 10E, 2L)

THE VILLIERS FLYWHEEL MAGNETO 25

The timing of the firing in relation to the position of the piston should now be checked. The engine should be rotated so that the contact-breaker points are just beginning to open when the piston should be $\frac{11}{64}$ in. before top-dead-centre. To adjust to this condition the base plate is moved to the left to advance and to the right to retard the timing after which the breaker is reset.

It may be necessary to repeat these operations until the gap and the position of the piston are correct when both locking screws D and E are tightened.

To lubricate the pivot of the rocker arm a fairly light grease is satisfactory. The oiling pad is treated by soaking it in molten grease which

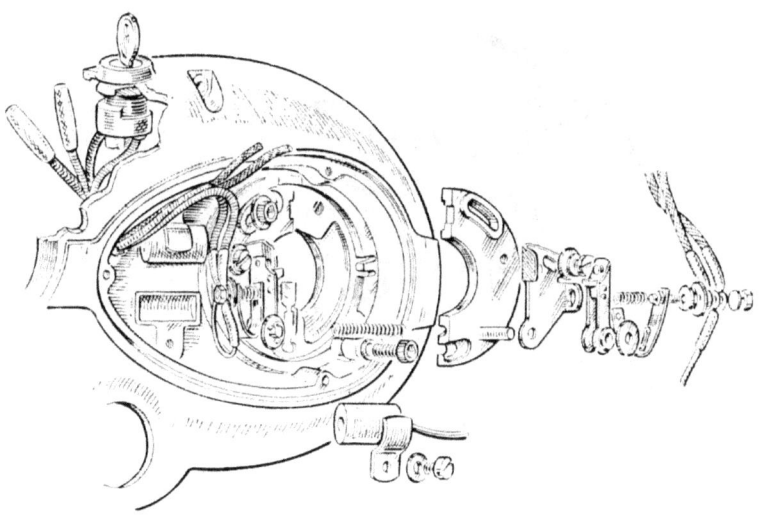

FIG. 20. CONTACT-BREAKER GROUP (MARKS 2T AND 3T)

has a high melting point and fixed so that it rubs on the cam at its highest point of lift. Lack of grease or bad positioning will lead to rapid wear of the fibre pad on the rocker arm, often resulting in a tiresome shrill squeak.

With the twin-cylinder Marks 2T and 3T engines, each has a separate ignition circuit energized by one of the coils on the armature plate. Each cylinder can be timed independently, because the contact-breaker assemblies are on separate base plates each being capable of rotation round the centre line of the ignition cam. The base plates should not be disturbed unless it is found necessary to alter the timing.

The contact-breaker assembly is shown in Fig. 20, and the point bracket, rocker arm, spring and connecting strip can be removed as a unit from the base plate by removing the split pin and point-bracket retaining screw.

When dismantling, it is most essential to remember the position of all the bushes, pins and insulating washers so that they can be reassembled correctly.

The base plate is held by three socket-headed screws (Fig. 21), but the timing is correctly set at the works and it normally needs no alteration.

To adjust the gap, the engine is rotated until the left-hand contact-breaker contacts are fully open which they will be when the left-hand (drive side) piston is at top-dead-centre. The left-hand point-bracket

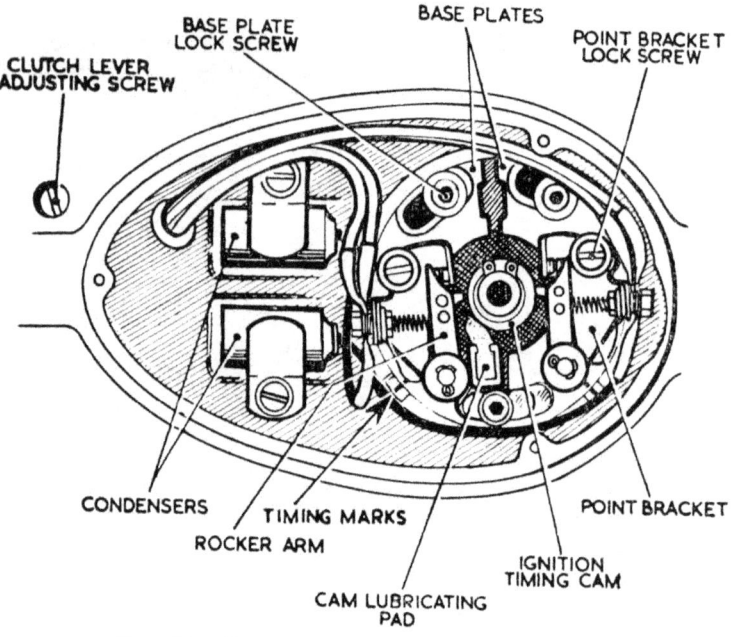

FIG. 21. CONTACT-BREAKER ASSEMBLY DETAILS
(MARKS 2T AND 3T)

lock screw is loosened, the gap is adjusted (using the feeler gauge) to 0·012 to 0·015 in. and the lock screw tightened up again. Do the same with the right-hand contact-breaker so that the right-hand piston on the magneto side is at top-dead-centre.

If the ignition must be retimed, it will be necessary to remove the solder found on the head of the three socket-headed screws. The gap setting having first been properly adjusted the engine is rotated until the left-hand piston is $\frac{3}{16}$ in. before top-dead-centre, then the lower socket-headed screw is loosened (Fig. 21) followed by the screw securing the left-hand contact-breaker bracket, which is rotated until the points just start to open. The base plate fixing screw is locked. The engine is now rotated until the right-hand piston is $\frac{3}{16}$ in. before top-dead-centre, when the

THE VILLIERS FLYWHEEL MAGNETO

right-hand contact-breaker base plate is adjusted until the points are just opening.

The timing of each cylinder is now rechecked, the bottom socket-headed screw is tightened and the other two screws are examined for security.

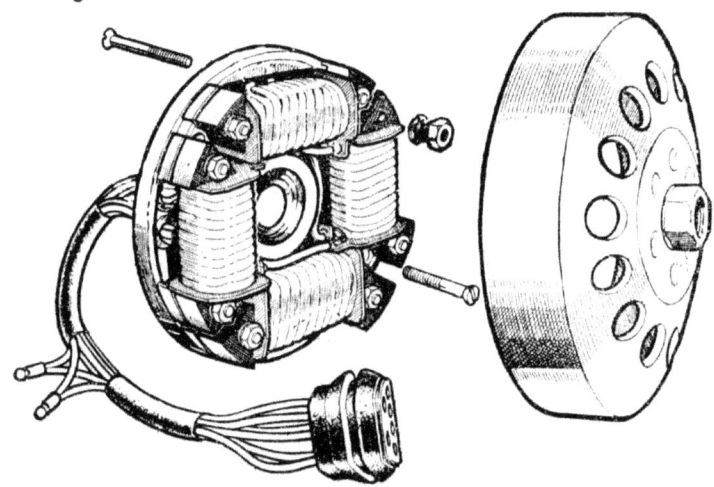

FIG. 22. ARMATURE PLATE AND FLYWHEEL GROUP
(MARKS 2T AND 3T)

With engines of this type the cylinder heads should be removed accurately to check the position of the piston in the cylinder.

The felt pad should occasionally be soaked in molten high-melting-

Engines	Before T.D.C.
"Junior" de-luxe	$\frac{1}{4}$ in.
1F, 2F, 4F, 6F	$\frac{1}{8}$ in.
10D, 11D, 12D, 9D	$\frac{5}{16}$ in.
29C, 30C, 31C, 6E, 7E, 8E, 2T	$\frac{5}{32}$ in.
1H	$\frac{5}{32}$ to $\frac{3}{16}$ in.
3T	$\frac{3}{16}$ in.
31A, 32A, 9E, 10E	$\frac{11}{64}$ in.
34A	$\frac{1}{8}$ to $\frac{5}{32}$ in.

point grease to provide lubrication between the cam and the fibre-heeled rocker arms. The two condensers are securely held by clips.

It is not wise to dismantle the two ignition coils which are in moulded cases with external screwed connexions (Fig. 22). It is, however, important to see that the connexions of the multi-pin socket and plug from the engine to the ignition coils and battery-charging contacts are kept tight and clean.

Where the unit has a self-starter fitted, no separate adjustment of the timing is possible. The base plate is in one piece. When the ignition timing of one cylinder is accomplished, the timing on the other cylinder is automatically correct.

Magneto Spark Timing. The correct ignition timing is most important as it affects smooth running and prolongs engine life. In the table on page 27 the distance before top-dead-centre of the piston is given at the moment when the magneto contact points should begin to open.

4 The Villiers electric lighting systems

BEFORE the Second World War, the Villiers lighting system was of the direct type from the flywheel magneto which incorporated lighting coils. The alternating current from these coils was led direct to the front and rear lamps in which light was available only when the engine was running. In order to provide light as a stand-by when the engine was stationary, a dry battery was fitted in some instances, but it needed frequent replacement.

Another system was to convert the alternating current to direct current by a commutator to charge an accumulator and this was known as the accumulator charging set. This system is now obsolete.

Another set aimed at providing stationary lighting was the dynamo charging set which incorporated a Westinghouse metal rectifier thus considerably simplifying the provision of direct current to the accumulator. It is doubtful whether any are still in use.

The modern system is to use a six-pole flywheel magneto to provide current for both ignition and lighting, either via a rectifier and battery or direct using a dry battery for the parking lights.

Engines Mark 4F and 6F. Two types of lighting equipment are available on these engines, one using a rectifier and the other supplying current direct to the lamps.

With the rectifier lighting, the alternating current coming from the lighting coils is changed to direct current when it passes through a selenium-type rectifier to charge a 6-volt 10 amp-hour battery. From the wiring diagram (*see* Fig. 23) the important circuits to study are from the rectifier and battery and the magneto and rectifier. The positive side of the battery is earthed to the motor-cycle frame and is thus in permanent contact via the frame, with the outer metal plate of the rectifier. The rectifier, which is hermetically sealed, can be fitted to any part of the frame so long as metal to metal contact is established and maintained.

When the headlight is in use and, say, a spot-light and electric horn as well, the output from the generator does not quite balance the load taken from the battery. It is important then to appreciate that if no daylight riding is undertaken, the battery will certainly have to be charged separately. If the motor-cycle has to be used when the battery is off for charging, the lead from the magneto to the rectifier *must be disconnected* and *insulated with tape*.

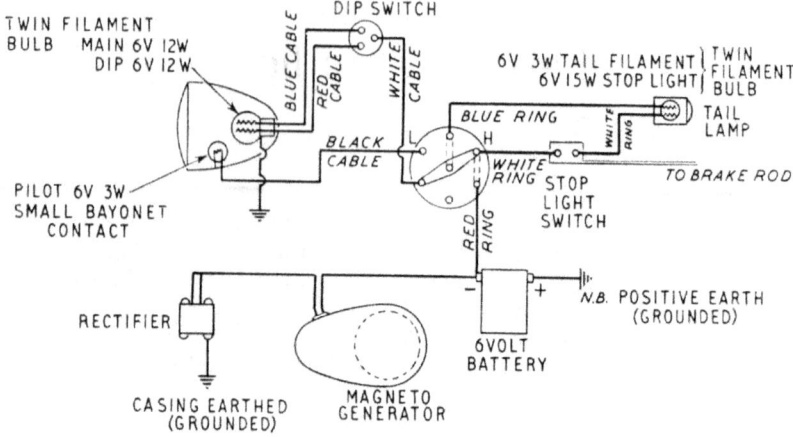

FIG. 23. WIRING DIAGRAM OF THE RECTIFIER-TYPE LIGHTING SET FITTED TO MARKS 4F AND 6F UNITS

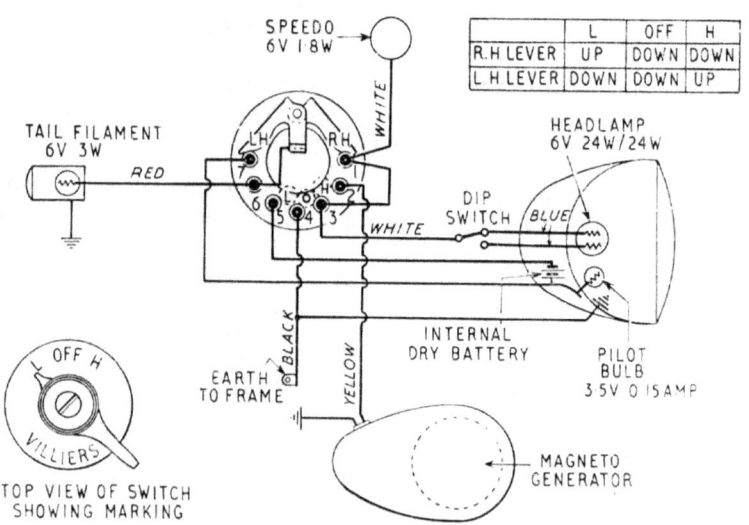

FIG. 24. WIRING DIAGRAM OF THE DIRECT-TYPE LIGHTING SET FITTED TO MARKS 4F AND 6F UNITS

THE VILLIERS ELECTRIC LIGHTING SYSTEMS

Mysterious rapid running-down of the battery is usually caused by incorrect fitting of the tail-lamp bulb. This must be put into its holder the right way round so that when the brake pedal is used the 18-watt filament stop-light comes on, but for parking or normal driving the 3-watt filament operates.

The battery must be given regular attention by being topped up with distilled water poured carefully into each cell until the acid level is seen at the top of the separators. The terminals should be kept clean, and there must be no corrosion beneath or around any joint which might otherwise appear sound. Close examination is called for.

With direct lighting (Fig. 24) the current is taken via the headlamp switch

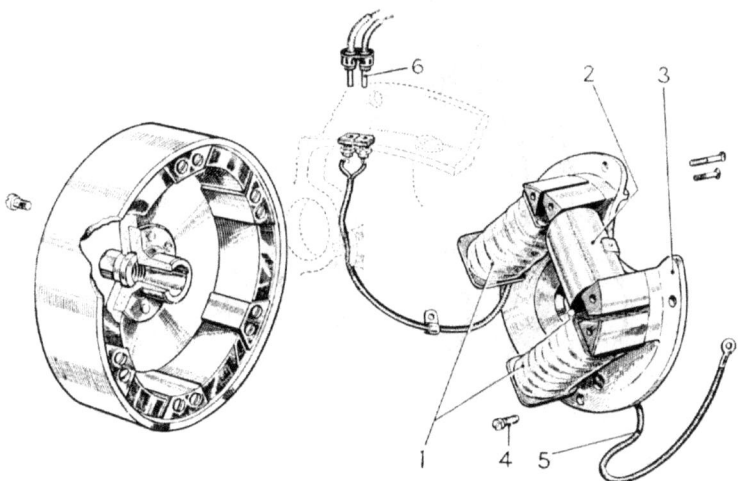

Fig. 25. Flywheel and Armature Plate (Marks 4F and 6F)

to the lamp, current for the parking light being provided by the dry battery (Ever-Ready Type 800) fitted in the headlamp shell. The design of the sets is quite different, so that the direct lighting set cannot be converted to a rectifier set by the addition of a rectifier. Because of the obvious advantage given by the rectifier unit, it is always advisable to specify this set when purchasing a new or second-hand machine.

MAGNETO COILS AND LEADS. The two lighting (1) and the one ignition coils (2) (Fig. 25) are fitted to the armature plate (3) which is held to the engine crankcase with four screws (4) using shake-proof washers. To remove the high-tension ignition cable leading from the coil to the sparking plug, it is unscrewed out of its socket at the top of the crankcase but care should be taken that the brass spring, pad and screw are not lost and that they are correctly replaced, noticing particularly that the brass pad is in full contact with the soldered disc on the outside of the ignition coil.

The low-tension lead (5) from the coil to the contact-breaker is passed through a passage way in the gearcase and crankcase. This lead is held in place with solder at the ignition-coil end and by a shoe at the other end which is secured by the low-tension terminal screw which also holds the condenser lead. If then the low-tension lead is to be removed it will have to be unsoldered from the coil. To permit the lead to pass through the

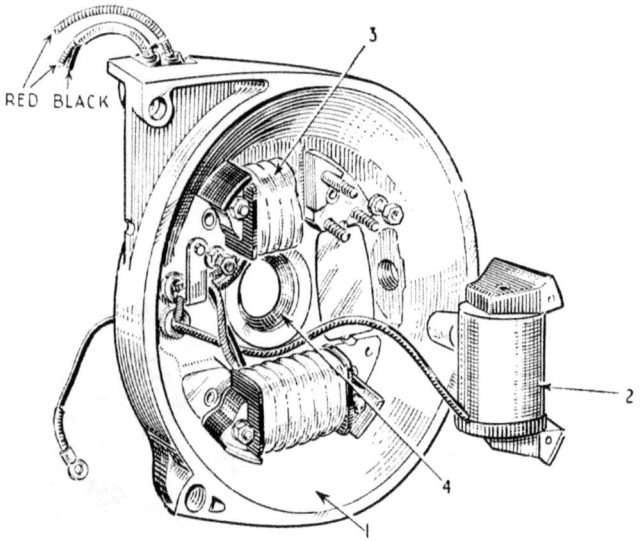

FIG. 26. ARMATURE PLATE FOR 12-VOLT LIGHTING COILS (MARKS 31A, 31C, 9E, 10E, AND 2L)

castings, where the coil and lead are taken out together, the shoe must be removed from the other end.

The leads from the lighting coils are taken to sockets on the clutch case via a twin cable (6) and if this cable is unfastened in any way, it is essential to make sure when replacing it that it passes through the slot in the coil platform so that it cannot foul the flywheel. The cable is secured by a clip screwed to the armature plate and then passes via the clutch case to the sockets.

Engines Mark 9E, 2L, 31C, 31A, and 10E. With these models, the magneto-generator is totally enclosed inside the cover on the right-hand side of the engine and comprises the flywheel, the armature plate 1 (Fig. 26) and the contact-breaker assembly and is available in 6-volt three coil form or as a 12-volt two-coil high-output type. The flywheel is held to the driveshaft by a key and secured on a taper by a single centre nut. The pole

THE VILLIERS ELECTRIC LIGHTING SYSTEMS 33

shoes and magnets are screwed to the flywheel and the whole assembly is balanced and magnetized after the final machining. The flywheel magnets should never need attention and nothing is to be gained by taking off the pole pieces or magnets. If, however, there seems to be a reduction in the magnetism, then the complete flywheel should be returned to the Villiers Service Department.

The armature plate is screwed to the right-hand crankcase and carries the ignition coil (2) and lighting coils (3). The high-tension lead connects to the ignition coil by way of a spring-loaded brass pad. With the 6-volt system the lighting coils are connected to cables which lead to sockets on top of the armature plate and in the case of the 12-volt system to leads which are fed through grommets in the plate. It is not wise to remove the pole pieces of the coils unless they are being renewed, because they are machined after they have been assembled to the plate. But on the other hand, all coils bought as spares are provided with the appropriate length of connecting lead and the pole pieces are, of course, machined, in which case it is important to see that there is a clearance of 0·012 in. to 0·015 in. between the pole pieces of the coils and those of the flywheel. If the engine is run before this check is made then damage may occur. When replacing the armature plate to the crankcase, the oil-seal (4) which is housed in the armature plate should be carefully refitted without damage being done to the knife-edge.

6-VOLT SET. This is available for rectifier or for direct lighting. The lighting switch ammeter and speedometer are contained within the head-lamp shell.

For rectifier lighting the three coils in the flywheel magneto provide the current for lighting and for charging the battery. The alternating current from the coils is converted to direct current by way of the selenium rectifier and it is well to know the manner in which the change-over is made. When the switch is in the "off" or parking position, one lighting coil only is in use and the battery is on charge. When the switch is in the "head" position the other two lighting coils are brought into circuit and as these are in parallel, the full output of the magneto is then obtained. With the switch in the "direct" position, the bulbs are connected directly to the two lighting coils thus allowing for an ample charge to be given even at the lowest engine speed.

The casing of the rectifier must not be in contact with any part of the motor-cycle frame and whatever insulating material is used (and it varies according to the manufacture of the motor-cycle) it must be carefully replaced if the rectifier is removed.

It is important to understand that provided the positive battery lead is properly insulated and the wiring is sound no damage will occur to the rectifier if the engine is in operation without the battery, but in order to prevent blowing of the bulbs, high engine speeds should be avoided if the switch is moved to other than the "direct" or "off" positions.

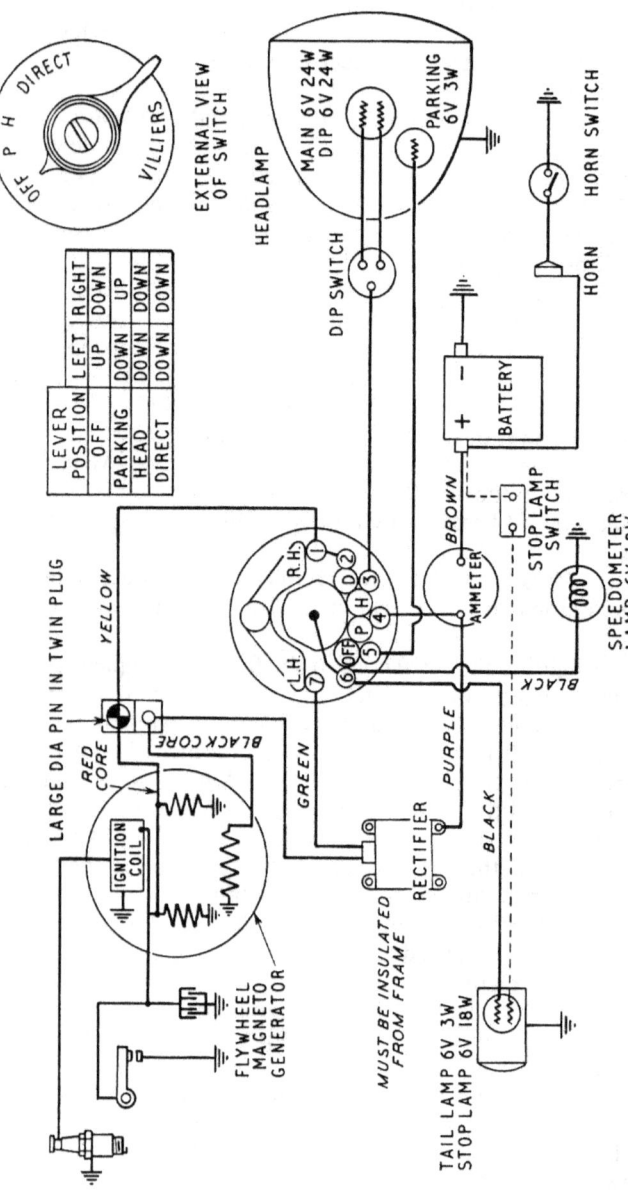

Fig. 27. Wiring Diagram for Rectifier Lighting, Using 6-volt Magneto-generator (Marks 31A, 32A, 34A, 31C, 9E, 10E, and 2L)

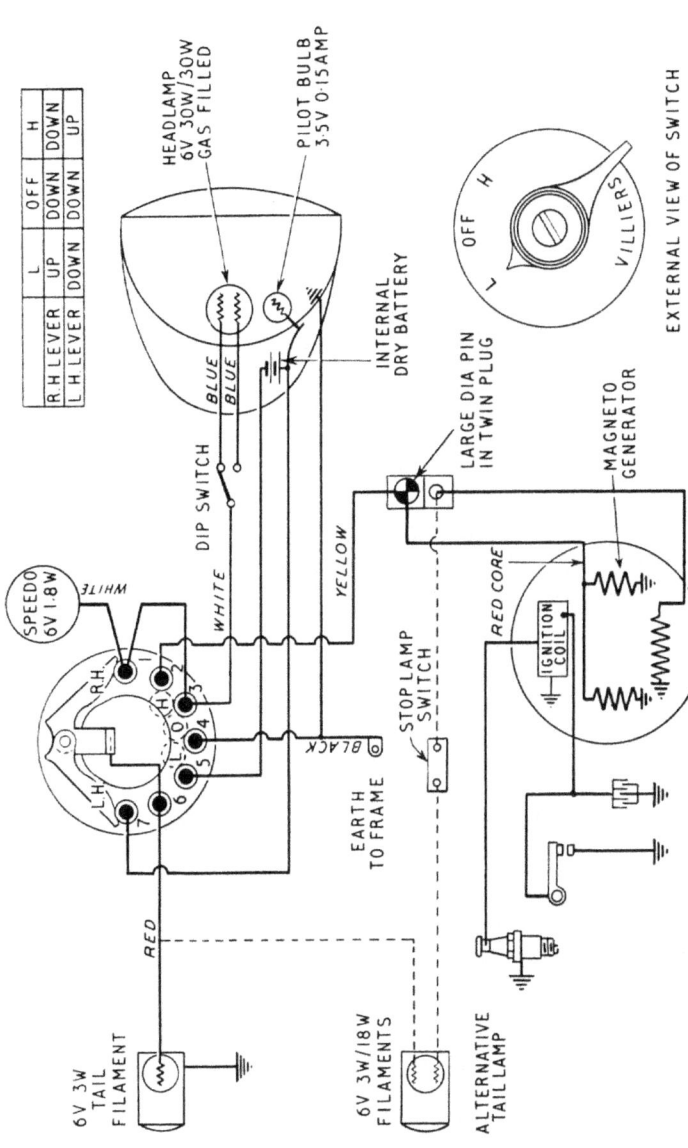

FIG. 28. WIRING DIAGRAM FOR DIRECT LIGHTING, USING 6-VOLT MAGNETO-GENERATOR (MARKS 31A, 32A, 34A, 31C, 9E, 10E, AND 2L)

The direct lighting set is used where it is not desirable to incorporate a battery on the machine. Two coils are used, the third for the stop-light or A.C. horn (Fig. 28). It will be realized that the main headlamp bulb is in use only when the engine is running, but in order to arrange for parking lights a dry battery is housed in the headlamp shell.

12-VOLT SET. The wiring circuit is shown in Fig. 29, but as the electrical

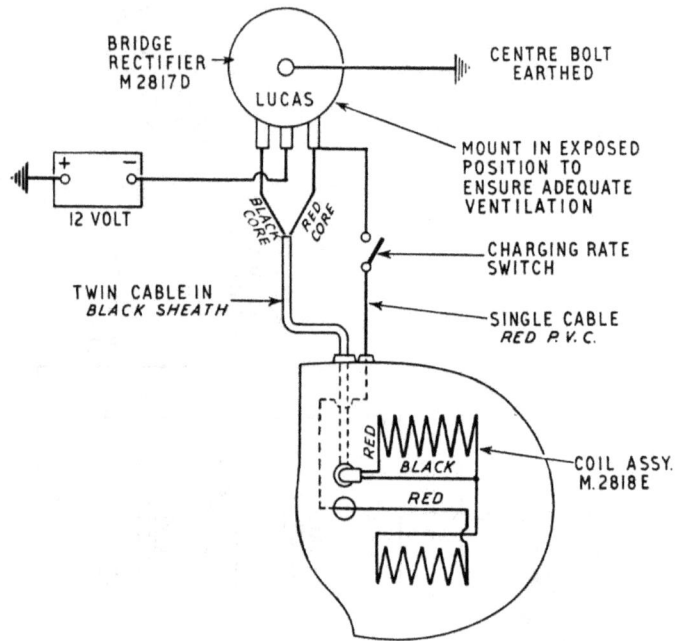

FIG. 29. WIRING DIAGRAM (BASIC CIRCUIT) FOR 12-VOLT MAGNETO-GENERATOR (MARKS 31A, 32A, 34A, 31C, 9E, 10E, AND 2L)

accessories used in conjunction with the magneto are supplied by the manufacturers of the motor-cycle, application should be made to them for any wiring diagram and replacement parts. If the engine is to be run with the battery disconnected it is important with the 12-volt rectifier lighting set to disconnect from the rectifier and insulate the black core of the twin-cable.

The battery is supplied by the makers of the machine and it is important to see that correct polarity is kept at all times as shown on the wiring diagram. The battery must be kept properly filled with distilled water.

Dismantling (*see* Fig. 18). First of all take off the cover by removing the three screws which will expose the contact-breaker assembly. Remove the nut from the point bracket pin so that the ignition-coil contact-breaker lead can be removed.

Take out the two slotted screws in the right-hand cover and the hexagon nut behind the armature plate near the front fixing lug. The right-hand cover is located on two hollow dowels in the armature plate and the cover may have to be eased off these dowels. The ignition-coil-contact-breaker lead terminal end will now pass through the slot in the housing but it is not wise to dismantle the contact-breaker cam, the contact-breaker points or the condenser.

Now comes the removal of the flywheel. The cam-retaining circlip is removed from the end of the crankshaft, preferably with the special pliers. The cam can now be taken off the shaft and the locating key removed so that the flywheel can be withdrawn from the crankshaft by turning the hexagon centre nut anticlockwise. This nut, after first slackening, will be found to tighten and if turning is continued the flywheel will now be pulled off from the tapered shaft. It is always well to use a proper Hammer-tight spanner rather than an open-ended spanner which might damage the hexagon nut. Keep the flywheel away from any metal parts but there is no need to place any metal bar as a keeper across the magnets.

The lighting lead plug is now disconnected from the twin socket on the armature plate and when this is removed, the flywheel locating key should be taken out so that no damage is done to the oil-seal. The high-tension terminal and lead are now unscrewed from the armature plate and the four slotted screws taken out after which the plate should come away.

Reassembly. This should not be difficult. The armature plate-assembly is fitted to the right-hand crankcase by the four countersunk screws and a spigot provides its correct positioning in the bearing housing. The crankcase oil-seal should certainly be renewed if necessary.

The faces of the armature plate and crankcase should be coated with Seccotine before fitting and care should be taken that the twin lighting lead and the low-tension lead are not trapped. The four countersunk screws are tightened in diagonal rotation and because the armature plate carries the full weight of the right-hand cover these screws must be tightly fixed. It is as well to lock them by lightly punching metal into the screw slot.

Then follows the fitting of the flyw c l k y into the crankshaft key-way, then the flywheel, taking care that the key is not pushed out of position and that the flywheel key-way engages properly. The centre nut is then tightened. The ignition cam key is now fitted followed by the cam while the flywheel is held in a strap wrench. The cam-retaining circlip is then fitted.

Having made sure the condenser is in its correct position and that its clip and screw are secure the right-hand cover can then be put on and held in position by the two countersunk screws and one stud which goes through the armature plate at the front end. The low-tension lead must be passed through the slot at the rear of the contact-breaker housing. Tap the cover into position on the hollow dowels in the armature plate, put in the two screws and the plain washer and nut and tighten up.

The contact-breaker base plate should be properly positioned on the pivot dowel and the fixing screw with washer in position, but this screw should not be locked until the ignition has been retimed. Reference to Figs. 18 and 21 will now enable the components to be properly reassembled on the contact-breaker point bracket which should be positioned between the fibre bush and the fibre washer.

The point bracket is then fitted over the rocker pivot-pin followed by the point-bracket fixing screw and the insulating and plain brass washers. The rocker arm is positioned on the pivot pin, taking care that the connecting strip is properly located on the raised pip on the back of the rocker arm. The rocker-arm spring is then fitted properly at one end on the point bracket pin and at the other end on the raised pip of the rocker arm. Lubrication of the rocker arm should be provided by light grease.

The rocker-arm-retaining washer is then fitted, followed by the split pin, but in order to avoid any sluggish movement of the rocker arm the washer must be free to rotate when the split pin is fitted. The washer is available in one of four thicknesses and if the correct washer is used then there will be no end float of the rocker arm yet it will move freely.

Information with regard to the proper setting of the points and the retiming of the ignition is given on pages 22–8. The high-tension lead is the last to be fitted, taking care that the felt washer is in its proper position on the pick-up terminal before screwing this terminal into the armature plate.

Engines Mark 2T and 3T. The ignition and battery charging circuits of the flywheel magneto-generator are each fed from two coils fixed to the armature plate on the right-hand side of the engine. The full wiring diagram is shown in Fig. 30, where it will be seen that the lighting equipment consists of the coils, a selenium rectifier and a battery. The selenium rectifier is used to convert the alternating current from the magneto lighting coils to direct current.

The rectifier is fitted into position by the manufacturers of the motorcycle, so that there is good ventilation all round. This point is important and the position should not be changed. The casing of the rectifier should not come into contact with the machine or it may be damaged. The central bolt which holds the rectifier is isolated from electrical connexions, which means that there is no need to see that a clean contact is made with the frame. It is not wise to loosen or turn the centre bolt which holds the rectifier or the sealing may be damaged.

It is most important *not* to run the engine with the battery disconnected unless the cables to the outer terminals of the rectifier are removed and properly insulated. If this is not done, the rectifier may be seriously

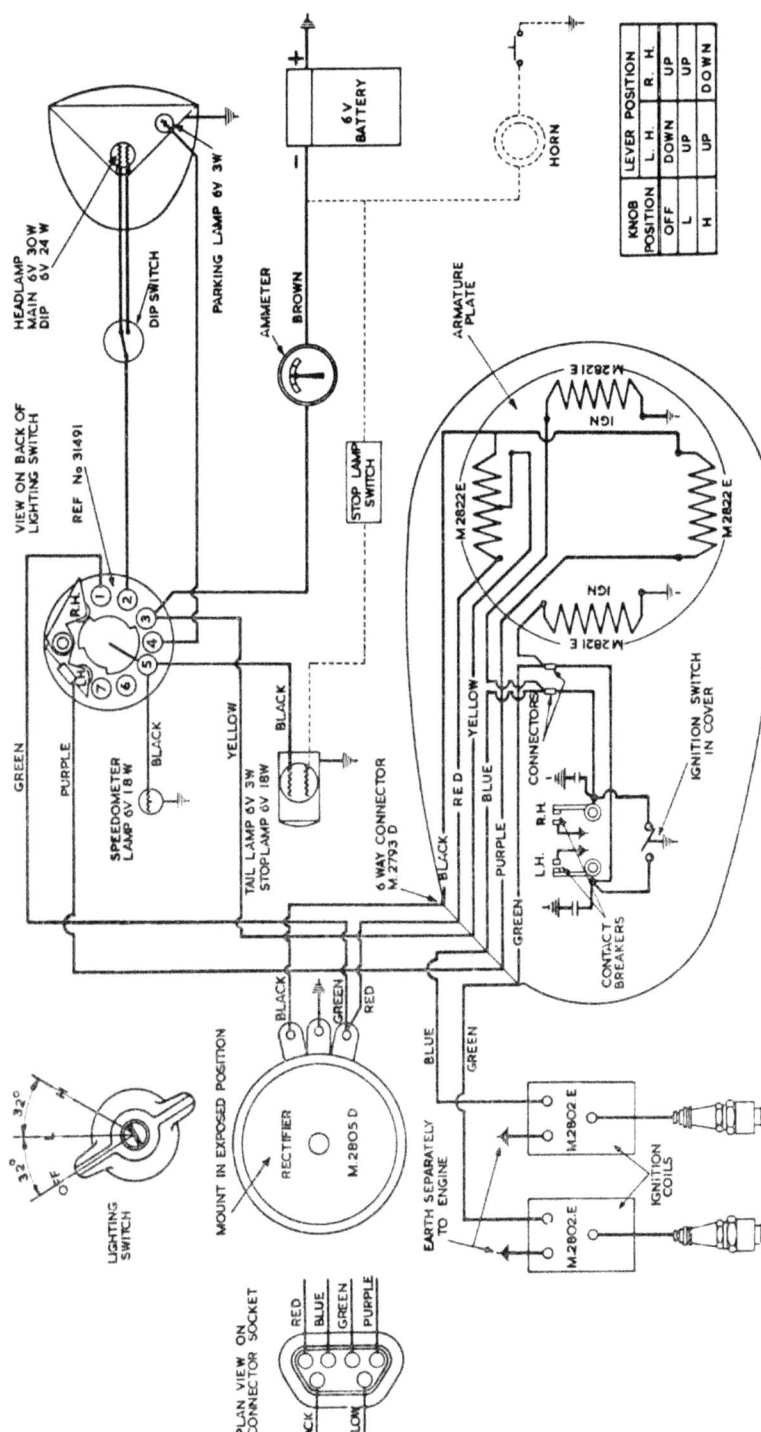

Fig 30. Wiring Diagram for Marks 2T and 3T

REPLACEMENT BULBS

Engine type	Lighting system	Head main	Head pilot	Tail main	Stop	Stop/tail	Parking	Speedometer
"Junior" de-luxe	Direct	6 V 1 amp SBC	4 V 0·3 amp MES	4 V 0·3 amp MES				
1F	Direct	6 V 18/18 W SBC	3·5 V 0·15 amp MES	6 V 3 W SBC				
1F	Rectifier	6 V 12/12 W SBC	6 V 3 W MBC	6 V 3 W SBC	6 V 18 W			
2F	Direct	6 V 12 W SBC	4 V 0·3 amp MES	4 V 0·3 amp MES				
2F	Direct	6 V 30/30 W SBC	3·5 V 0·15 amp MES	6 V 3 W SBC				
10D 6E	Rectifier	6 V 24/24 W SBC	6 V 3 W SBC	6 V 3 W SBC	6 V 18 W			
10D 6E	Direct six-pole	6 V 24/24 W SBC	3·5 V 0·15 amp MES	6 V 3 W SBC				
4F 6F	Rectifier	6 V 12/12 W SBC	6 V 3 W MBC	6 V 3 W SBC	6 V 18 W			
4F 6F	Direct	6 V 30/30 W SBC	3·5 V 0·15 amp MES	6 V 3 W MBC				
8E, 12D, 29C 30C	Rectifier	6 V 24/24 W SBC	6 V 3 W MBC	6 V 3 W MBC		6 V 18/3 W		6 V 0·17 amp MBC
8E, 12D, 29C 30C	Direct	6 V 30/30 W SBC	3·5 V 0·15 amp MES	6 V 3 W MBC				6 V 0·17 amp MBC
9E, 2L, 31C, 31A, 32A, 34A, 10E	Rectifier	6 V 24/24 W SBC	6 V 3 W MBC			6 V 18/3 W		
2T 3T	Rectifier	6 V 30/24 W SBC				6 V 18/3 W	6 V 3 W MBC	5 V 1·8 W

THE VILLIERS ELECTRIC LIGHTING SYSTEMS

damaged. As an alternative, the lighting switch can be left in the "H" position, although here again if the engine is allowed to rev rapidly the lamps may be overloaded and the rectifier damaged. Note that the centre lead goes to earth and should not be altered.

When the switch is in the "L" or "off" position, one lighting coil only is in use. This provides a charge to the battery which is more than enough to balance the consumption of the headlamp, pilot tail-light and speedometer bulbs. If the switch is in the "H" position the other lighting coil is brought into circuit and as this is connected in parallel the full output of the generator is then provided.

The Battery. Regular care should be given to see that the battery is always kept in good condition. Many troubles can be traced to the battery's being allowed to get into bad order although the battery is rarely blamed until everything else has been checked over. It is important, for instance, to see that the correct polarity is maintained and here you should refer again to the wiring diagram (Fig. 30). Distilled water should be added about once every fortnight in the summer and once every month in the winter through the filler cap of each cell, to bring the level of the liquid just above the top of the separators. Tap water or water containing organic matter should never be used: neither should acid be added unless it has been spilled from the battery. Even then it is best to go to a battery service depot for testing.

It is important to keep the battery terminals clean and free from corrosion.

5 Villiers carburettors

THE purpose of the carburettor is to supply a mixture of suitable proportions of petrol and air to the cylinder so that when compressed and fired by the spark at the plug from the magneto expansion takes place to provide the power.

The principle of carburation is as follows (Fig. 31). Liquid petrol issues

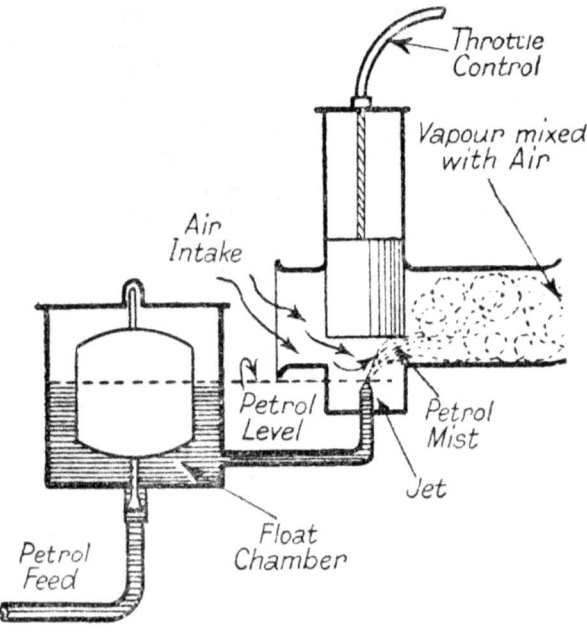

FIG. 31. DIAGRAM EXPLAINING THE PRINCIPLE OF CARBURATION

through a minute nozzle or jet into a stream of rapidly moving air, by which process it is converted from liquid fuel into a highly atomized vapour. The upward stroke of the piston sucks this air stream through the carburettor, and the quantity of the petrol-air mixture that is allowed to pass into the engine is controlled by the throttle slide. The strength of the mixture depends upon the proportion of fuel emerging from the jet, and the air passing through the carburettor.

In most instruments other than Villiers the size of the jet is fixed, so that a set quantity of petrol with air, giving a proved suitable proportion, is constantly fed to the engine.

In the Villiers instrument, the amount of petrol that is allowed to issue from the jet is automatically proportioned to the amount of air passing it, from which it will be seen that this instrument covers a wide range of varying engine conditions.

The Villiers carburettor thus gives a perfectly and automatically adjusted mixture over the whole range of throttle openings and this adjustment is achieved by means of its compensating action which is very simple.

Being entirely automatic in operation, the instrument requires only one lever to control it. Such an arrangement is better than having one air and one throttle slide, each controlled by a separate lever, because with the latter arrangement, the rider is always over-correcting his mixture.

In the Villiers instrument, the one lever opens and closes the throttle and, at the same time, enlarges or reduces the size of the jet by means of a taper needle attached to and working with the throttle.

The practical application of the carburettor is to supply the correct mixture of petrol and air under all conditions. As the fuel enters the float chamber the float rises and stops the flow when the required level is reached and it is kept at this level by a lever resting on the float which checks the fuel coming in by lifting a needle valve. In the bottom of the centre-piece is the jet through which the fuel enters. Into the top of the centre-piece is fitted the tapered needle. If the air supply is closed by the throttle then the largest diameter of the needle cuts down the fuel supply, but if the throttle allows more air to pass so the diameter of the needle also permits more fuel to pass. The choice of needle position, needle taper and jet size ensures the correct mixture of fuel and air no matter what the throttle opening.

Type "Junior" 6/0. The "Junior" 6/0 carburettor (Fig. 32) is fitted to the Marks 1F, 4F and 6F (early) engines. The "Junior" fitted to the "Junior" de-luxe and Mark 2F is of the same design but without the oil-wetted gauge filter and strangler.

DISMANTLING. The milled threaded ring (1) at the top of the carburettor is unscrewed and pulled upwards taking with it the throttle (8) with the cable attached. In the centre of the throttle is a slotted screw (5) which lowers the needle if it is turned clockwise to give a weaker setting, and vice versa. One should be careful not to adjust it so that too much petrol is coming through because this merely adds to running costs and tends to build up carbon in the engine. The setting which is too rich also leads to four-stroking. It is only necessary to give the adjuster screw a half-turn at a time. If the adjuster screw seems to be slack in its thread, it should be taken out and the end opened just enough to make the screw fit tightly

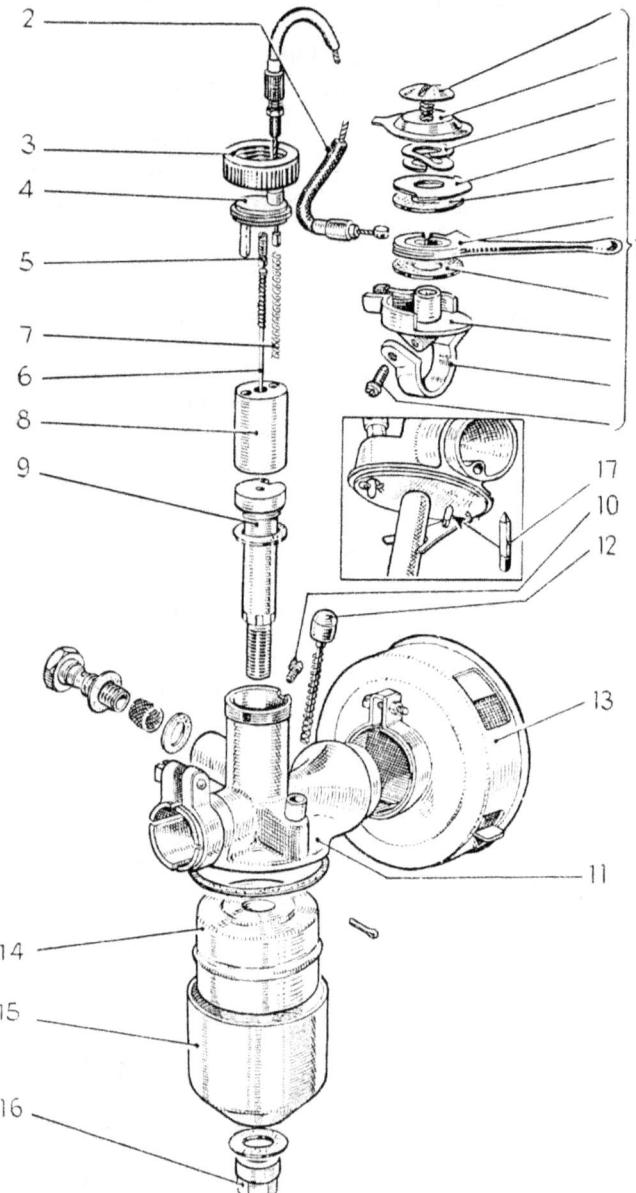

FIG. 32. COMPONENT PARTS OF THE "JUNIOR" TYPE 6/0 CARBURETTOR FITTED TO MARK 1F, 4F AND 6F (EARLY) ENGINES

1. Handlebar control and clip
2. Control cable
3. Top ring
4. Top disc with guide peg
5. Taper-needle adjuster
6. Taper needle
7. Throttle spring
8. Throttle
9. Centre-piece with jet
10. Centre-piece locating screw
11. Carburettor body
12. Tickler
13. Air filter
14. Float
15. Float chamber
16. Bottom nut
17. Fuel needle

You will see that it is split at the lower end, and each half should be prised open so as to provide sufficient friction to prevent the screw loosening.

If you wish to remove the taper needle, (6) the adjuster (5) should be taken out so that the needle can be pushed up from beneath. When replacing, take care that the spring is in the right position beneath the head, because if it is not, the movement of the adjuster will not affect the position of the needle which will be loose and will cause erratic carburation.

If it is found necessary to remove the centre-piece and fuel needle from the body of the carburettor the nut (16) beneath the float chamber is unscrewed to allow the fibre washer, the float chamber (15) and float (14) to come away. It is important to remove the small locating screw (10) which is below and at the rear of the petrol-pipe union and to replace it in the same position later. The centre piece (9) can now be pushed through the throttle-slide hole. The fuel needle (17) should now be taken out. The slit needle lever is a fixture and no attempt should be made to remove it.

This fuel needle controls the admission of the petrol-oil mixture into the carburettor and when the float rises fully the needle should cut off the supply. The upper end of the needle is tapered and if the carburettor has been causing trouble from flooding or slight dripping, then possibly the needle seating or the seating in the bush may be worn. Unless this wear is excessive, it can be corrected by grinding-in the needle valve using a little grinding paste. The needle valve should be held on the seating and "twiddled" between the finger.

The level of the petroil mixture in the float chamber is determined by the shape of the fuel needle lever. It is not wise to alter the shape because it may well give a higher level of the petroil and this would certainly affect the economical and smooth running of the engine. The distance between the underside of the carburettor body and the top of the float should be between $\frac{3}{16}$ in. and $\frac{7}{32}$ in.

It is not usually necessary to remove the tickler (12) unless it is felt that the air vent holes need to be examined for clogging. It is removed by taking out the split pin taking care not to lose the spring. One vent hole is at the bottom of the hole into which the spring fits and the other in the side of the tickler cap.

REASSEMBLY. It is most important that the carburettor be correctly assembled otherwise annoying troubles may be experienced.

The fuel needle is first fitted into its seating and the fuel-needle lever held so that the needle is secure and the centre-piece can be passed between the two prongs on the lever. The centre is next fitted (with the fibre washer first) in such a manner that the small locating screw (10) can be properly positioned in the slot in the head of the centre-piece. Then the float is replaced on to the centre-piece; care must be taken that the fuel needle lever has not become bent. Next to be replaced are the float chamber, the fibre washer and the retaining nut which should not be overtightened.

Be quite sure that the carburettor body is pushed well home on to the manifold stub so that there is no air leakage which will lead to difficult starting and erratic running.

Type S.12. The carburettor fitted to the later engines, Marks 4F and 6F is the Type S.12 (*see* Fig. 33).

DISMANTLING. To remove the throttle slide (1) it should be fully opened and the screw (2) holding the flat top-cap removed, after which the throttle can be drawn out. Care must be taken not to bend or scratch the taper needle (3). The throttle can be taken from the cable (4) by releasing the tension on the throttle spring (5) from the handlebar control and then lifting the nipple of the cable out from the slot in the slide. The taper needle can be taken out after the spring clip (6) has been moved over to one side.

Unless the jet is badly worn there is no reason to remove the jet block (7) and the fuel needle (8) from the body, but if it is felt to be necessary, then a special tool is needed to remove the jet block which is screwed into the body of the carburettor. When the float chamber (9) the float (10) and the fuel needle lever (11) have been taken off, then the fuel needle and the fuel needle bush (12) can be removed and examined. The bush, however, is screwed into the carburettor body and unless it is felt that a replacement is necessary it should not be moved.

To remove the tickler (13) a circlip (14) is taken off at the bottom after which the tickler and the spring can be pulled out from the top. If the jets require to be cleaned, then the main jet (15) is screwed out from the float chamber, and the air compensating jet (16) from the carburettor body. The latter should not require cleaning if the air filter (17) has been kept in good order and in position.

REASSEMBLY. Although it should be easy to reverse the dismantling process, there are certain important features to observe. The first is to screw in tightly the two jets (15 and 16) and the fuel needle bush (12) otherwise they can easily jiggle loose and eventually cause serious trouble. The fuel needle (8) must be put in to the bush with point upwards and the fuel lever (11) fitted on to its hinge pin. When the float is properly in position it should not be affected by the tickler but if the fuel needle lever has in any way been bent, it should be reset, so that between the lower face of the carburettor body and the top of the float there is a vertical distance of $\frac{7}{32}$ in.

It is the easiest thing in the world to lose or to forget the inclusion of the float-chamber sealing washer (19) which must not only be properly fitted but must be in good order and seated properly in the recess in the body of the carburettor.

The float chamber should be tightened up by hand not by a spanner otherwise the threads may be damaged.

The taper needle goes back into the throttle slide and is held by a spring clip in the right groove. The throttle spring and cable are then replaced.

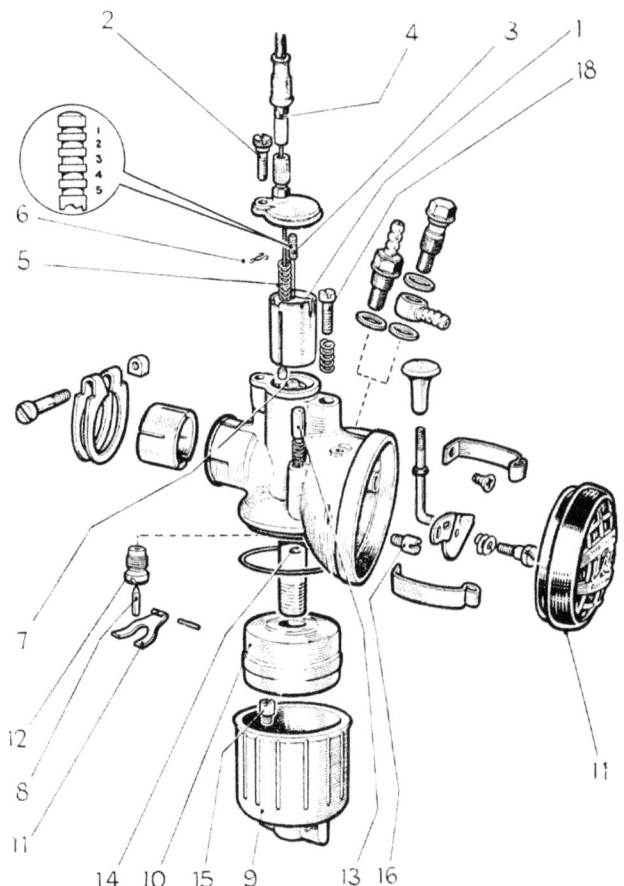

FIG. 33. COMPONENT PARTS OF THE TYPE S.12 CARBURETTOR
(FITTED TO MARKS 4F AND 6F)

1. Throttle slide
2. Top-cap screw
3. Taper needle
4. Throttle cable
5. Throttle spring
6. Taper needle retaining clip
7. Jet block
8. Fuel needle
9. Float chamber
10. Float
11. Fuel needle lever
12. Fuel needle seating bush
13. Tickler
14. Circlip screwing tickler
15. Main jet
16. Compensating jet
17. Air filter
18. Air by-pass screw
19. Float-chamber sealing washer

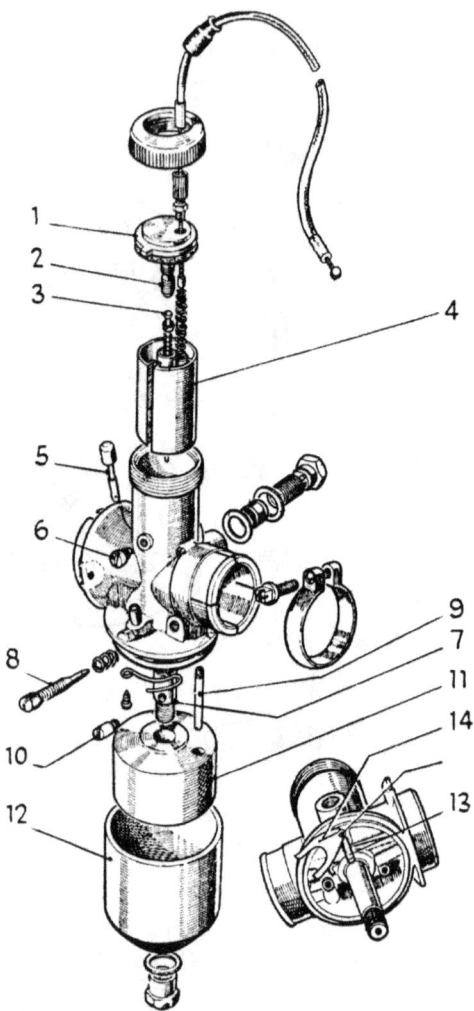

Fig. 34. Component Parts of the Type S.19 and S.25 Carburettors as Fitted to Marks 12D, 30C and 31C Engines

1. Top disc
2. Needle adjusting screw
3. Needle
4. Throttle slide
5. Tickler
6. Throttle guide screw
7. Centre-piece
8. Pilot-needle jet
9. Pilot jet
10. Main jet
11. Float
12. Float chamber
13. Fuel needle
14. Fuel needle lever

VILLIERS CARBURETTORS

The throttle slide is guided into the top of the carburettor body so that the needle fits into the jet block and then follows the refitting of the top cap and its screw.

RESETTING. As mentioned before the makers have selected the correct main and air compensating jets and the right taper needle to give the best results, and the only adjustment which should be necessary is the setting of the taper needle and the adjustment of the air by-pass screw (18). At the top of the taper needle (3) are five grooves and the position of the needle

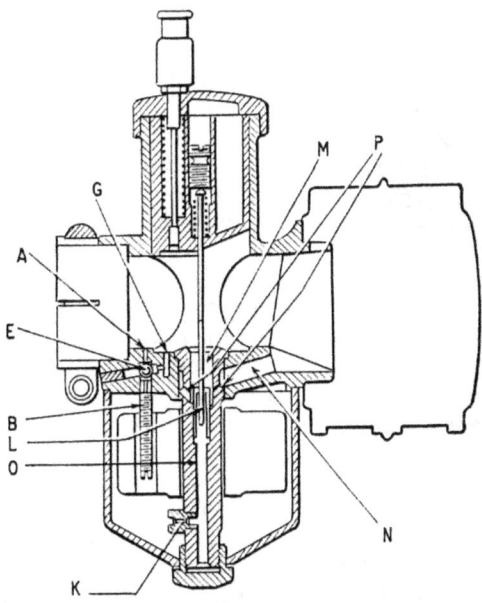

FIG. 35. SECTION OF THE TYPES S.19 AND S.25 CARBURETTORS

controls the mixture strength between quarter and three-quarters throttle. The higher the number of the groove, the richer is the mixture, so that groove (1) is the weakest, but the usual position is groove (3). The speed of the tick-over is adjusted by the cable adjusting screw.

The function of the air by-pass screw is to allow the mixture to be adjusted between the closed and the quarter-open throttle position; screwing it in makes the mixture richer and unscrewing it makes the mixture weaker.

Type S.19. The Type S.19 carburettor (Fig. 34) is used on the Marks 12D, 30C and 31C engines, but it has proved so efficient and economical that it is also used with certain variations on most of the current models. It has two jets—a main jet and a pilot jet. When the engine is idling the pilot jet provides the fuel, but as the throttle is opened the fuel comes first from the pilot progression hole and then from the main jet system.

THE PILOT JET. When the machine is idling there is a particularly high engine suction across the pilot outlet hole A (Fig. 35) and this causes petrol to be drawn up from the float chamber through the pilot tube B to the pilot outlet hole. While the petrol is being sucked up through the calibrated pilot jet, filtered air is drawn into the mouth of the carburettor through passage C (Fig. 36) by way of the variable air jet D and is then thoroughly mixed with the fuel in the chamber E. The screw F is used to alter the size of the pilot air jet and in turn the mixture strength, i.e. it is turned clockwise to enrich the mixture and anticlockwise to weaken it. As the throttle is opened so the suction on the pilot outlet hole is lessened but the suction over the progression hole at G (Fig. 35) is increased. The purpose of this progression hole is to ensure a continuity of the fuel supply during the change over from the pilot jet to the main jet. It provides for excellent acceleration and prevents what is known as a flat spot.

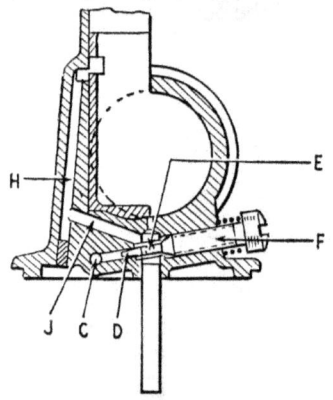

FIG. 36. THE COMPENSATING DEVICE OF THE TYPES S.19 AND S.25 CARBURETTORS

One will appreciate that if the throttle is closed while the engine speed continues high, as might occur when running downhill, the pilot system recieves the full engine suction and fuel would flow into the engine via the pilot outlet hole. As the engine would not be using this fuel it would tend to build up in the crankcase and cylinder and lead to serious four- or eight-stroking as the throttle was opened. This is obviated through the use of an automatic air bleed to the pilot jet, the operation of which depends upon the matching of two slots, one in the carburettor body and one in the throttle slide. When the throttle slide is shut the two slots are in line, thus allowing air to flow from the front of the carburettor down to the throttle slide and through passages H and J (Fig. 36) into the pilot system. This means that the high depression on the pilot system is not possible. On the other hand, in all other throttle positions the two slots are not in line and therefore no air can pass to the pilot system by way of these slots.

MAIN JET. The main jet system comes into operation when the throttle is opened beyond the idling and the progression positions. The calibrated main jet K (Fig. 35) is fitted in the centre-piece and petrol is now drawn from the float chamber through this jet and via the needle jet L into the chamber M where the petrol is atomized by the air drawn in from the mouth of the carburettor along the orifice N to enter the centre-piece O through the four small holes at P. This comparatively rich pre-mixed petrol-air combination then flows into the main mixing chamber where it comes into contact with the main air stream. Because the taper needle is fixed to the throttle slide, the effective size of the needle jet L depends upon the position of this throttle slide, and the needle and needle jet are of dimensions specially chosen to give the optimum carburation over the whole range.

TUNING. It is important to follow the directions given here, because it is quite easy to upset the adjustment of one part of the carburettor by subsequent adjustment. Tuning must therefore be done in proper sequence and as there are four adjustments, each has its particular effect on a given throttle range and must be regarded as being satisfactory only over that particular part of the range. Prior to the actual tuning adjustment it is most essential to make sure that the carburettor is clean, the air filter is not obstructed, the supply of fuel is not checked, there are no air leaks at the joint and that there is a good "fat" spark at the plug. Tuning should therefore be done in the following order.

(a) *Main Jet: Throttle Range Three-quarters to Full.* With the correct main jet 10 (*see* Fig. 34) the engine at full throttle and in top gear should show ample power, should not detonate or run better with the strangler slightly closed. If it does fail in these respects a larger main jet should be fitted. On the other hand, if the engine four-strokes even occasionally or gathers momentum when the petrol has been turned off, then it is an indication of an over-rich mixture and a smaller jet should be tried. I always like to try it out at fairly high engine speeds in neutral when, at full throttle, the engine should have a tendency to four-stroke. It is important to have a correct main jet otherwise speed and acceleration are bound to be disappointing.

(b) *Pilot Jet: Throttle Range Closed to One-eighth Open.* Testing now is done with the motor-cycle stationary and the engine running at the desired idling speed, the idea being to have a weak mixture consistent with steady idling and yet giving satisfactory acceleration. On the other hand, if the mixture is too rich, trouble will be experienced because of the fuel build-up in the crankcase when the throttle is closed and the engine is still turning over fairly fast. To make the mixture richer, the pilot adjuster screw F (Fig. 36) should be screwed in and to weaken unscrewed.

(c) *Throttle Cut-away, Throttle Range One-eighth to One-quarter Open.* If you examine the throttle slide 4 (Fig. 34) you will see that there is a cut-away portion on the carburettor inlet side and this influences the depression on the main jet system. The throttle is marked with a number which gives the amount of cut-away in sixteenths of an inch. The throttle with the greater cut-away will give weak mixtures over that particular throttle range and it follows that if the acceleration seems to be poor the throttle should have a smaller cut-away; if the engine tends to four-stroke when the throttle is closed then a larger cut-away should cure the trouble.

(*d*) *Needle Adjustment: Throttle Range One-quarter to Three-quarters Open.* Adjustment here is easy because the needle (3) (Fig. 34) is adjusted by a screw (2) found on the underside of the throttle slide cover. It is screwed down to weaken the mixture and up to enrich. The mixture strength over the ordinary cruising speed is controlled by the needle and should be accurately adjusted in order to obtain satisfactory acceleration combined with fuel economy. After the adjustment has been made it is usually advisable to check the pilot adjustment to see whether that has been affected by the other adjustments.

CHANGING THE TAPER NEEDLE. If the top ring is unscrewed the throttle can be carefully pulled out from the body. The small slotted screw (2) seen in the centre over the top of the throttle is the adjuster already referred to and if this is removed, then the needle with the spring can be pushed up from underneath, but do make sure when replacing the needle that its collar and spring are in the right position.

REASSEMBLY. The centre-piece (7) (Fig. 34) is a press fit in the body and it is not wise to remove it. Before reassembling see that all the various parts and vent holes are clean and that any damaged washers have been renewed. See that the main jet (10) is properly positioned in the side of the centre piece and the float (11) the right way up as marked. Then put on the float chamber (12) with the large fibre washer at the top followed by the fibre washer and nut at the bottom. This nut should be tightened up firmly but not with undue force or the thread on the bottom of the centre piece may be damaged.

As the throttle is guided back into the body the taper needle should be carefully located in the top of the centre-piece making use of the guide screw (6) for its correct positioning. Then follows the cover or top disc which is held by the threaded ring.

See that the carburettor is pushed right on to its manifold stub to make the join air-tight, and that it is upright. Difficult starting and erratic running are frequently caused by air getting in at the manifold stub via the four slots over which the securing clip is fitted. Do not forget to clean out the fine-mesh filter gauze which will be found in the petrol pipe connexion.

An efficient air filter is usually fitted to this carburettor and to provide the necessary strangling there is a hand-operated slide or shutter. Take care that the filter is kept clean and properly maintained.

Type S.22. The Type S.22 carburettor (Fig. 37) is fitted to Mark 2L and 3L engines. The operation, dismantling, reassembling and tuning apply as for carburettor Type S.19 but with the following differences.

The adjustment of the needle (1) is done by moving a spring clip (2) into one of five grooves at the top of the needle. The higher the groove used the weaker the mixture. The centre groove (No. 3) is regarded as normal. The idea is to make the adjustment such that whilst the machine has good acceleration, its fuel consumption is not excessive.

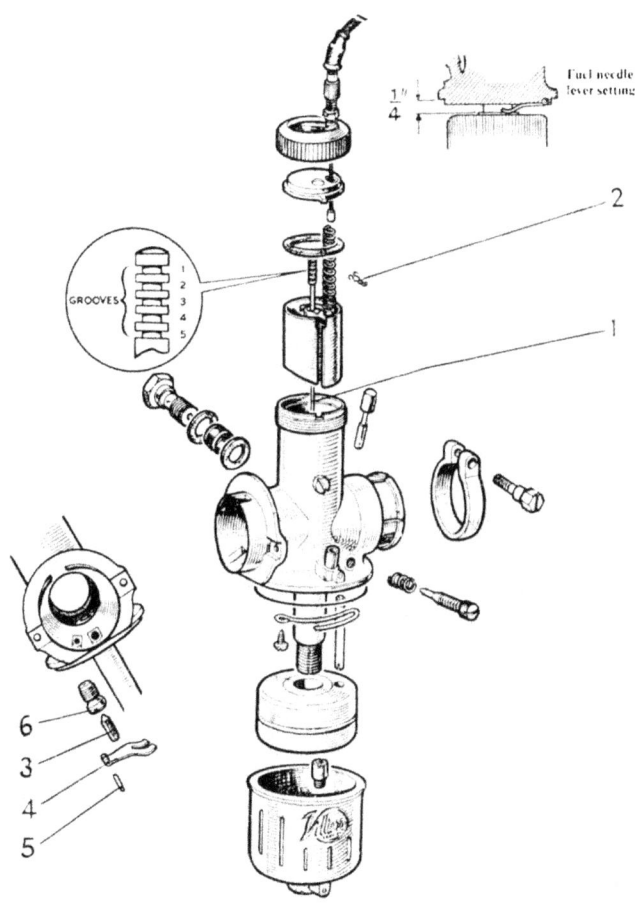

FIG. 37. COMPONENT PARTS OF THE TYPE S.22 CARBURETTOR AS FITTED TO MARKS 2L, 2T, AND 3T ENGINES

1. Needle
2. Needle-securing clip
3. Fuel needle
4. Fuel-needle lever
5. Fuel-needle lever hinge pin
6. Fuel-needle bush or seating

The taper needle position can be changed by moving its retaining spring to one side.

To change the fuel needle (3) the float chamber and float are removed after the retaining nut at the bottom has been unscrewed. The fuel needle lever (4) is released by pulling out the hinge pin (5) which acts as its pivot, after which an examination can be made of the efficiency of the seatings of both the needle and its bush (6) which can also be removed. It is important when reassembling to see that the distance between the top of the float and the underside of the carburettor body, as allowed by the position of the fuel needle lever, is $\frac{1}{4}$ in. (*see* Fig. 37).

The carburettor fitted to the Mark 2T and 3T engines is the Type S.22/2. It has a large air filter as standard and to provide for strangling from cold an air slide is fitted within the carburettor throttle (*see* Fig. 38). This is operated either by hand by moving a knob at the top of the carburettor, or by a remote-control lever on the handlebars. Be sure that the filter is kept clean at all times, or petrol consumption will be heavy and the engine will form excessive carbon.

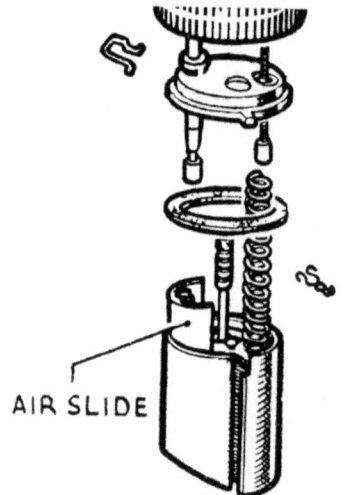

It is important to remember that the centre-piece in this model forms an integral part of the carburettor body.

When reassembling, see that the main jet is firmly screwed into the float chamber, otherwise follow out the procedure explained under Type S.19.

FIG. 38. POSITION OF THE AIR STRANGLER SLIDE IN THE TYPE S.22/2 CARBURETTOR

Type S.24. Used on Mark 11D, 7E, and 8E engines, this carburettor is similar to the Type S.19, but it has a large choke and the throttle is positioned by a guide peg attached to the throttle chamber.

Type S.25. Designed for use on Mark 31A, 8E, 9E, 10E, 1H, and 2H engines the Type S.25 carburettor is a larger model of the Type S.19 to suit the larger capacity engine. The same instructions as to operation, dismantling and tuning therefore apply.

Type S.25/5. This carburettor is similar in design and construction to the Type S.19, but it has a felt sealing washer in place of the air filter and a knob-operated strangler slide built in the carburettor body as in the Type S.22/2 carburettor instead of a strangler slide in the air filter.

Affixes 1, 2 and 3. The affixes to the Types S.19/1, S.19/2, S.19/3 (also S.22 and S.25), do not signify any differences in design or operation but merely whether the model is fitted with a strangler or not. Thus S.19/1

without strangler, S.19/2 with strangler slide and hand-operated knob, and S.19/3 with cable-operated strangler slide.

CARBURETTOR TYPES, THROTTLE AND NEEDLES

Type of engine	Type of carburettor	Throttle No.	Needle taper (degrees)
Junior de-luxe	Junior	J7	2
1F	Junior type 6/0	8	$2\frac{1}{2}$
2F	Junior	J8	$2\frac{1}{2}$
4F }	Early Junior type 6/0	J120	$2\frac{1}{2}$
6F }	Later S.12	1	2
11D	S.24	2	$3\frac{1}{2}$
12D	S.19	2	$3\frac{1}{2}$
29C	S.25	3	$3\frac{1}{2}$
30C	S.19	$2\frac{1}{2}$	$3\frac{1}{2}$
31C	S.19	$2\frac{1}{2}$	$3\frac{1}{2}$
31A	S.25	3	$3\frac{1}{2}$
32A/4	S.25	4	$3\frac{1}{2}$
33A/4 } 34A/4 }	Amal 389	$3\frac{1}{2}$ (Amal)	D in No. 3 groove
2L	S.22	$2\frac{1}{2}$	$3\frac{1}{2}$
7E	S.24	3	$3\frac{1}{2}$
8E	S.24 or S.25	3	$3\frac{1}{2}$
9E	S.25	3	$3\frac{1}{2}$
10E	S.25	3	$3\frac{1}{2}$
1H	S.25	3	$3\frac{1}{2}$
2H	S.25/5	3	$3\frac{1}{2}$
2T	S.22/2	$2\frac{1}{2}$	$3\frac{1}{2}$
3T	S.22/2	$2\frac{1}{2}$	$3\frac{1}{2}$

6 Operating, handling and maintenance

THE running of your machine, its cost of maintenance and its useful life will depend a great deal on the manner in which it is used and maintained. The purpose of the information given in this chapter is to enable the owner to obtain the best possible results from his Villiers-engined motor-cycle.

LUBRICATION

It is most important that you use the correct types of oils and greases in the approved manner.

Engine. The drip-feed system, as originally adopted, of supplying oil to the engine is now practically obsolete. It consisted of a hand-operated pump which drew oil from a tank and fed it to the engine via a sight drip-feed.

A later system, as applied to the Marks S1, S2, and S3 engines, but now discontinued, depended upon the pressure built up in the crankcase on every down-stroke of the piston. It was an excellent system and gave good results.

However, the simplest and best method and that now universally adopted, is the "Petroil System" in which a fixed quantity of oil is mixed with a fixed quantity of petrol. With a new engine the proportions are usually one part of oil to 16 parts of petrol and after the engine has been run-in one part of oil to 20 parts of petrol will provide proper lubrication.

As the engine depends entirely upon this oil for lubrication it is important that it should be thoroughly mixed with the petrol. If possible this should be done before the petroil mixture is put into the tank of the motor-cycle but if this is not convenient then the petrol should be put into the tank first and then the oil. The machine should then be rocked from side to side in order to mix the oil as well as possible.

Petrol Service Stations now cater for the two-stroke engine by supplying the fuel already mixed, the pump being adjustable so that whatever proportion of oil to petrol is required can be supplied.

It is unwise to be careless about the oil-petrol ratio because if too much oil is used the plug will foul up, the engine will four-stroke and eventually excessive carbon deposits will build up in the engine to cause loss of power and other troubles. On the other hand insufficient oil will bring about premature wear of the moving parts and eventually serious damage will result.

OPERATING, HANDLING AND MAINTENANCE 57

If the engine is not to be used for, say twenty-four hours, it is always a good plan to turn off the petrol tap while it is running and allow it to run the carburettor dry. Starting troubles may occur if oil settles out in the carburettor bowl.

As to the oil to use there is little difference in quality between the well-known makes but it is advisable to keep to one brand and not to mix two different makes.

Gearbox

Engine mark	Brand and grade of oil	Instructions
4F 6F	Castrol D (SAE 40)	Take out oil level and oil filler plugs (Fig. 39); take machine off its stand; pour in oil until it runs out of oil level plug: screw plugs in firmly
9E 2L 31C 31A 32A 34A 10E	Castrol XL (SAE 20W/50)	Remove filler plug (and combined dipstick) (Fig. 40). Oil should be poured in until the level reaches the notch in the dipstick which should rest in its hole and *not* be screwed down. The machine should be on level ground. Every 5,000 miles the old oil is drained out via the drain plug and new oil added to the correct level
2T 3T	Castrol XL (SAE 20W/50)	See above and Fig. 41. Be sure not to over-fill: oil capacity of gearbox is 1·2 pints
	CHAINCASE LUBRICATION	
9E 2L 31C 31–34A 10E 2T 3T	Castrolite (SAE 10W/30)	Remove both oil level and filler plugs. (Figs. 40 and 41). Pour oil in until it starts to run out of baseplug hole. Let surplus drain out and replace both plugs firmly. Change oil every 5,000 miles. Do not over-fill

General. The speedometer drive (where fitted) is lubricated by the gearbox oil. Bowden control cables should be lubricated regularly to maintain free action and to stop rusting.

HOW TO HANDLE THE ENGINE

Starting Up. If a battery is fitted, make sure that it is connected up. If the battery is not in use for some reason or other, then the rectifier must itself be disconnected. If this is not done, the rectifier may well be seriously damaged. The gear lever should be in the neutral ("N") position and if there is any difficulty in shifting the lever to another position, then this

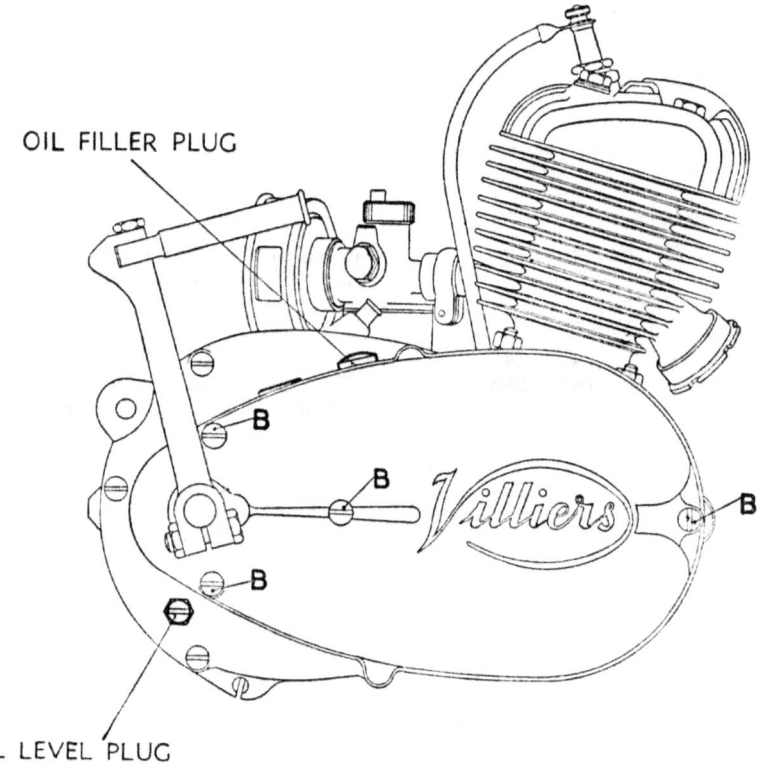

FIG. 39. MARK 4F ENGINE, RIGHT-HAND SIDE
Remove items marked *B* for access to flywheel

can often be assisted by rocking the machine backwards and forwards as the gear lever is being moved.

Be sure that the petrol tap is in the "on" position and the ignition switch (where fitted), also switched on. If the engine is cold, then the carburettor should be flooded with petrol by pushing down the "tickler" and at the same time closing the strangler shutter. The idea is to provide the carburettor with a rich mixture to make starting easy.

Open the throttle lever or twist grip about one-third and push down

OPERATING, HANDLING AND MAINTENANCE 59

sharply on the kick-starter, or depress the self-starter switch. As soon as the engine fires, the throttle should be moved so that the engine is nicely ticking over and as the engine gets warmer, so the strangler is opened to

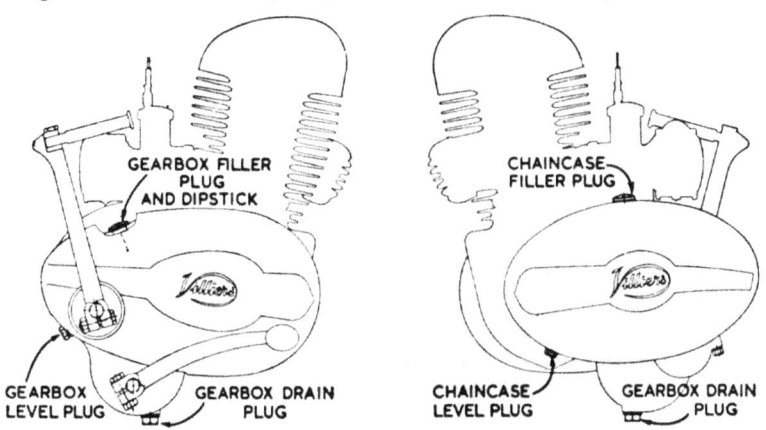

FIG. 40. POSITION OF OIL LEVEL PLUGS ON THE MARKS 2L, 31A, 31C, 9E, AND 10E UNITS

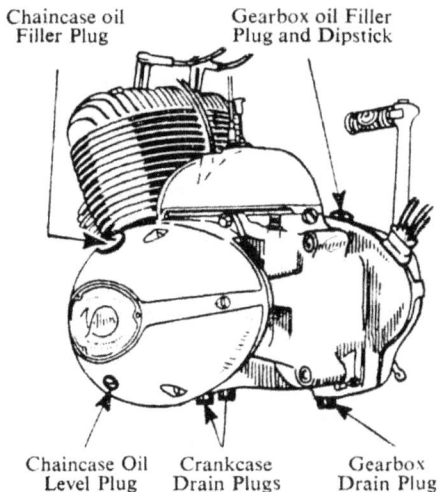

FIG. 41. OIL FILLERS AND DRAIN PLUGS ON THE MARKS 2T AND 3T ENGINE UNITS

allow a greater ingress of air. It is important to make sure that the strangler is not kept closed under normal running conditions, although in very cold weather, the strangler shutter may well have to be kept say half-shut until the engine has warmed itself up.

It is important when the engine is hot neither to flood the carburettor nor close the strangler because if this is done the engine will be flooded with petrol, and the mixture will be so out of balance that the spark will not be able to ignite it.

Poor Starting. If the engine refuses to start, it is a good plan to turn off the petrol, open the strangler fully and also the throttle and then turn over the engine several times, the idea being to throw out of the cylinder and crankcase any excessive petrol. It is probable that the engine will start before it is necessary to turn on the petrol tap.

If even then the engine refuses to start, take the sparking plug out and it will probably be found wet with petrol, in which case it will mean that the crankcase has still a considerable quantity of liquid mixture in it. In such a case it may be wise to take out the drain plug found at the bottom of the crankcase, and then to turn the engine over before the plug is put back in order to blow out this excess mixture.

If after trying this out, the engine still does not start, then it would be well to check up from the chart shown on page 90, starting with the spark at the plug and then the fuel supply.

Stopping the Engine. The engine can be stopped by closing the throttle right down or by switching off the ignition (where a switch is in operation) or by turning off the petrol, so that the further rotating of the engine uses up all the petrol mixture in the carburettor. This is advisable if the machine is not likely to be used for, say, twenty-four hours. By doing this no oil can collect in the bowl of the carburettor to cause starting difficulties.

On the Road. When the engine has been successfully started and warmed up, you should sit astride so that both feet are firmly on the ground. The clutch is then freed by pulling up the appropriate control lever, usually found on the left handlebar. The gear lever is then moved by hand or by foot, according to type, to the low-gear position so that when the clutch lever is slowly released, the motor-cycle will move forward. At the same time open the throttle gradually and so provide a smooth take-off without stalling the engine.

Accelerate by opening the throttle to about 10 or 12 m.p.h. when the next higher gear should be engaged by freeing the clutch, closing the throttle somewhat and then moving over the gear lever quite firmly to its next position. The clutch lever is then released and the throttle opened so that the machine will gather speed. It is important to make the gear changes firmly yet smoothly so that the engine neither labours nor races away.

The function of the gearbox is to provide variations between the speed of the engine and the rear wheel. In bottom gear the number of revolutions of the engine to each revolution of the back wheel is greater than in top gear and that is why one changes down on steep hills to a lower gear so that the engine revolutions will be maintained while the road speed of the machine becomes less.

The right way to change down from a high to a lower gear, is to release the clutch and adjust the throttle so that the engine speed is *increased* to keep it in step with the low-gear ratio after which the lever can be moved firmly over into the lower gear position.

Gears are to use, and when climbing a hill or in heavy traffic nothing is gained by keeping the top gear in use. The operation of the machine is much more pleasant if a lower gear is brought into operation before it is actually needed.

It is bad practice to lower the road speed by "slipping the clutch," which will show excessive wear in a short time and will lead to excessive clutch slip.

It may be found that on a new engine the gearbox seems somewhat stiff but this does not indicate that it has been incorrectly fitted or that any internal adjustment is necessary. The stiffness soon wears off and if one is careful in changing gear in the early stages, there will be nothing to worry about.

The Mark 2T (SFR and SR engines) can be started in either direction, but it is important that the first-gear position only is operated when the engine is running in the reverse direction.

Running-in. If you want an engine to have a long life, give a first-class performance and to call for only minor adjustments, then it is vitally important that the new engine should be properly "run-in."

The period during which an engine should be nursed is usually given at 500 miles, but for the best results and a long-lasting smooth-running engine, the period might well be extended to 1,000 miles. Although the various bearing surfaces are of a high production standard, they are comparatively rough and also tight and if because of excessive speed or overloading the new engine overheats or the surfaces become excessively hot, then wear which otherwise would not have taken place is most likely.

During this period, it is never wise to open the throttle fully, accelerate the engine under a light load or allow it to race. Indeed, with a two-speed machine, it would not be wise to exceed 20 m.p.h. in top gear and 12 m.p.h. in low gear. With a three-speed gearbox, the speed should be kept down to 30 m.p.h. in top gear, 18 m.p.h. in second gear and 12 m.p.h. in low gear. With a four-speed box, then the speeds which should not be exceeded, are 40, 24, 20 and 10 m.p.h. When the engine has been properly "run-in," then, with a four-speed gearbox (for instance, Mark 2T and Mark 3T engines) the maximum speeds may well be increased after 500 to 1,000 miles up to 50 m.p.h.; 1,000 to 1,500 miles up to 60 m.p.h.; 1,500 to 2,000 miles maximum speeds for short bursts; extended full throttle running should not be indulged before, say, 2,000 miles have been recorded.

RECOMMENDED LUBRICANTS (REGENT/TEXACO)

Villiers Unit (c.c.)		Engine Oil	Petroil Ratio	Gearbox Oil	Chain-case Oil
Mk. 3K	(50)	Motor Oil 2T	20 to 1	Havoline 30	—
Mk. 2F	(98)			—	Thuban 140
Mks. 4F, 6F	(98)			Thuban 140	—
Mks. 12D, 11D/4	(122)			Thuban 140	Thuban 140
Mks. 8E, 8E/4	(197)			Thuban 140	Thuban 140
Mk. 9E	(197)			Havoline 30	Havoline 20
Mk. 2L	(175)			Havoline 30	Havoline 20
Mk. 31C	(148)			Havoline 30	Havoline 20
Mks. 29C, 30C	(147)		20:1 (1st 500 miles 16:1)	Thuban 140	Thuban 140
Mk. 1H	(225)		20:1	Havoline 30	Havoline 20
Mk. 2T	(250)		20:1 (1st 500 miles 16:1)	Havoline 30	Havoline 20
Mk. 3T	(324)		20:1	Havoline 30	Havoline 20

RECOMMENDATIONS (CASTROL)

Engine

Castrol two-stroke oil (16:1), or Castrol XL (20:1). (16:1 is ½ pint of oil to 1 gallon of petrol.)

Gearbox

Models in and prior to 1956: Castrol D; otherwise use Castrol XL (SAE 20W-50) (including 4-speed models). Norman motor-cycles models 30C and 8E require Castrol D, and "Nippy" models Mark IV require Castrol XL.

Chain Case

Castrolite (a new formula multi-grade oil with viscosity range 10W/30).

Clutch Case

Castrol D (Junior de luxe model).

Grease

Castrolease LM, or high melting-point lithium grease required for most applications; use graphited grease for transmission chains.

RECOMMENDATIONS (MOBIL)

Engine

Mobil Mix—TT (16:1); this contains anti-rust addition.

Gearbox and Chain Case

Mobilube C 140 or GX 140, or GX 90 (most readily available and up to date) suitable for both.

Grease

Mobilgrease MP (multi-purpose) or Multigrease Special (with 3 per cent molybdenum disulphide added).

RECOMMENDATIONS (SHELL MEX & B.P.)

Engine

BP2 Two-stroke Oil (20:1). For a "Starmaker" racing engine use BP Racing SAE 50 (a castor-based oil).

Gearbox and Chain Case

BP Gear Oil SAE 140 for gearbox lubrication. Models using SAE 30 engine oil would require BP Energol SAE 30 or BP Super Viscostatic 10W/40 or 20W/50 for chain case lubrication.

Grease

For all applications: BP Energrease L2 (lithium-based).

RECOMMENDATIONS (ESSO)

Engine

Esso two-stroke (2T) (16:1).

Gearbox and Chain Case

Esso Extra (20W/30) suitable for both.

Grease Point

Multipurpose H for general use.

During the first 500 miles, special care should be taken with regard to lubrication, not only for the engine, gearbox, chaincase and speedometer cable, but also those other many surfaces which will certainly be properly protected only by the use of adequate quantities of oil such as Bowden cables, external rubbing surfaces, hubs and so on. It is also well to check up all nuts, bolts and screws to see that they are still secure. It is a double insurance after the first 500 miles to drain the chaincase and gearbox and refill with new oil of the right grade. At the same time it might be found advisable to adjust the carburettor setting to make it rather more economical of mixture and also to check over the plug gaps, contact-breaker points and ignition timing (*see* routine work in Chapter 7).

7 Adjusting and overhauling

MANY motor-cyclists derive a great deal of pleasure from carrying out their own adjustments and routine maintenance. Unless he is qualified, however, it is unwise for the amateur to attempt to carry out complete overhauls and this work is best left to the skilled mechanics employed by reputable motor-cycle service depots.

The following notes should enable all Villiers engine owners to do their own adjustments and routine overhauling with little or no difficulty.

The Tool Kit. A standard kit of tools accompanies all Villiers engines and they should always be carried on the machine. The kit usually consists of screwdriver and feeler gauge for contact-breaker adjustment, a larger screwdriver for general purposes, a plug spanner and probably a carburettor spanner. If you intend to do rather more than the usual simple adjustments then you will probably need a Hammer-tight spanner for the flywheel, an exhaust-nut spanner, an extractor for the self-starting rotor and possibly a spanner for the clutch cap nut; these are obtainable from the Villiers works through your local agent. You should also provide yourself with a hammer, a stout pair of wire-cutting pliers, a small good quality adjustable wrench and a good pressure-fed oil can. Other small tools you may require should be added as the need for them arises.

Routine Attention. Matters concerned with specific components as opposed to the engine itself will be found on pages 43–54 (carburettor), pages 23–6 (ignition), and pages 29–41 (lighting set).

EVERY 500 MILES. Where an air cleaner (Figs. 42 and 43) is fitted to the carburettor it is important to keep it clean and under particularly dusty running conditions it should be washed out every 250 miles. The cleaner should be removed, washed in petrol and then left to dry, after which it is dipped into clean oil or petroil and left for a while for most of the surplus to drain off. Those cleaners which have a specific list of instructions for overhaul should be dealt with accordingly.

Although it is not always necessary, it is also usually advisable to look at the contact-breaker points every 500 miles. They may need slight adjustment to ensure the correct gap (*see* page 22) and they must of course be kept quite free from oil.

During this check up, the oil level in the gearbox or chaincase should be inspected by taking out the oil-level screw or checking up on the dipstick

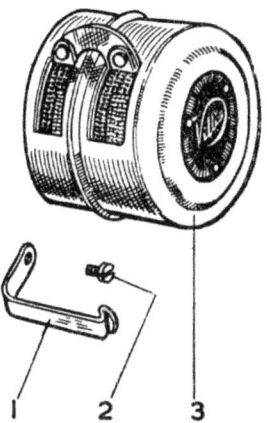

FIG. 42. THE STANDARD AIR CLEANER
1. Air filter clip
2. Clip screw
3. Filter incorporating air strangler

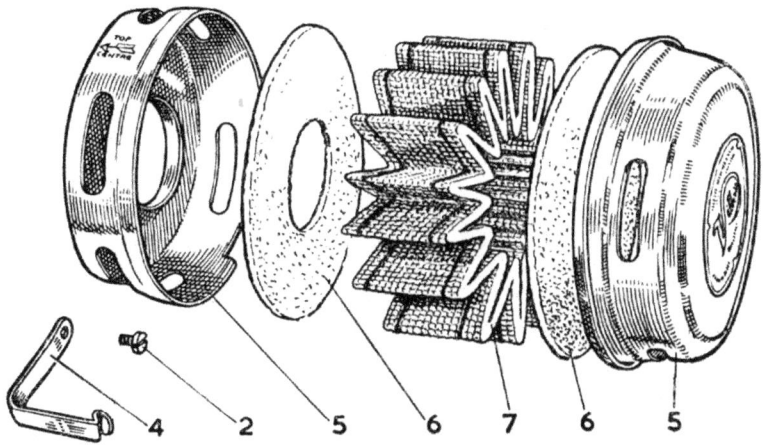

FIG. 43. THE "1100" AIR CLEANER

The Star element (7) collects the dust and has to be cleaned or renewed

2. Clip screw
4. Air filter clip
5. Filter end caps (two)
6. Felt sealing washers (two)
7. Star element

(*see* page 57). If necessary, top-up with the same make and grade of oil currently used.

EVERY 2,000 MILES. This is a suitable period for removing carbon deposits, a job known as "decarbonizing." This is dealt with in detail on page 71. Generally it is not necessary at this stage to remove the cylinder barrel and the piston. It is, however, important to take off and clean the exhaust pipe and silencer and to clean and reset the sparking plug points.

EVERY 4,000 MILES. It may or may not be necessary at this stage to remove the cylinder barrel to examine the cylinder bore and the piston. If one feels that everything is in order then it is best to leave well alone.

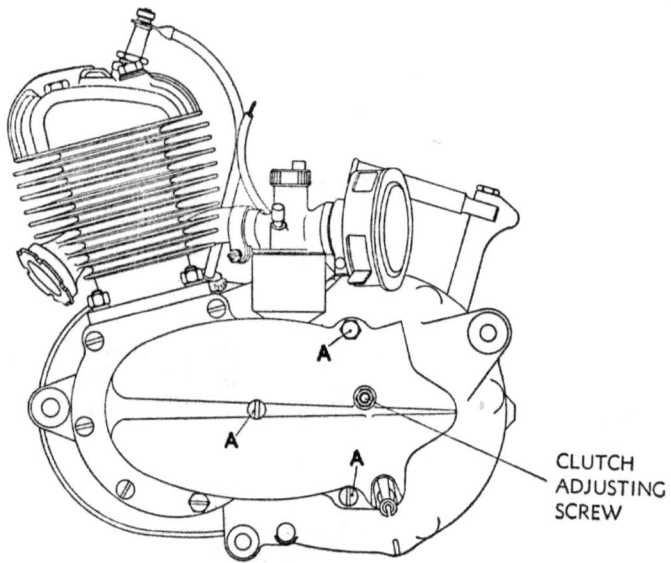

FIG. 44. MARK 4F ENGINE, LEFT-HAND SIDE
Remove screws marked *A* for access to contact-breaker

EVERY 5,000 MILES. Drain the gearbox and/or chaincase by taking out the drain plug at the bottom, doing this preferably when the engine is warm, so that as much of the old oil and sludge will come away. Where no plug is fitted to the chaincase then the front cover has to be taken off. After draining the plugs are put firmly back and fresh oil of the same brand and grade poured in to the appropriate level.

GENERAL. Go over all bolts, nuts and screws to see that they are not shaking loose. See that the joints between the cylinder head and barrel, crankcase and barrel, and the crankcase components are secure and that there are no oil leaks.

Clutch and Gear-control Cable Adjustment (Engines Mark 4F and 6F). Correct adjustment of these cables is most important. There must be from $\frac{1}{16}$ in. to $\frac{1}{8}$ in. movement between the lever and the cover and if at any time the lever touches the cover, then the clutch corks will wear rapidly. The clutch lever is adjusted by moving the screw shown in Fig. 44. When the engine is new or the clutch has recently been recorked it will be necessary to watch this point carefully. Frequent adjustments will be called for because of the "bedding down" of the surfaces.

The clutch control cable should be adjusted to leave $\frac{1}{16}$ in. If because of improper adjustment this degree of slack is not provided, then the clutch

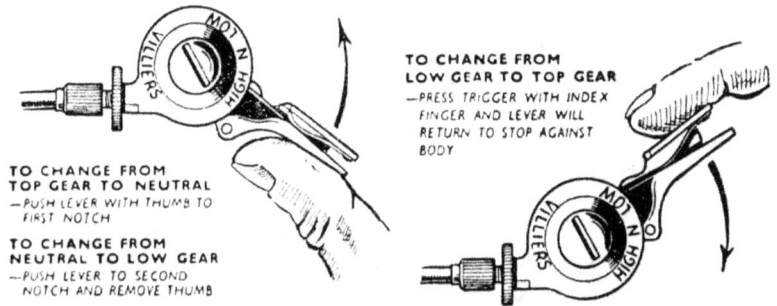

FIG. 45. OPERATION OF THE GEAR LEVER CONTROL OF THE MARK 4F TWO-SPEED GEARBOX

will not engage properly, slip will ensue and cause endless trouble and excessive wear. If the engine side cover is removed to inspect the contact-breaker or when an adjustment to the clutch lever has been carried out, it will be necessary to readjust the clutch cable.

It is of greater importance to maintain correct adjustment of the gear control cable, for if this is not done the gears will not stay in proper engagement and in some instances may be damaged.

The two-speed gearbox on the Mark 4F engine is controlled via a Bowden cable with the lever on the right-hand handlebar. The three gear positions—high, "N" neutral and low—are indicated on the cover plate of the lever as shown in Fig. 45 which also explains gear-changing procedure.

The Mark 6F engine has a foot-operated gear change (Fig. 46) with neutral in the central position, "up" for bottom gear and "down" for top gear.

Correct adjustment of the handlebar gear control cable is vital. There must be $\frac{1}{16}$ in. slack in the cable when the lever is in the "high" position in order to be sure that the gear is fully taken up and that the spring which holds the gears in the "high" position is in full operation.

There is ample adjustment provided on the cable, one point being on the

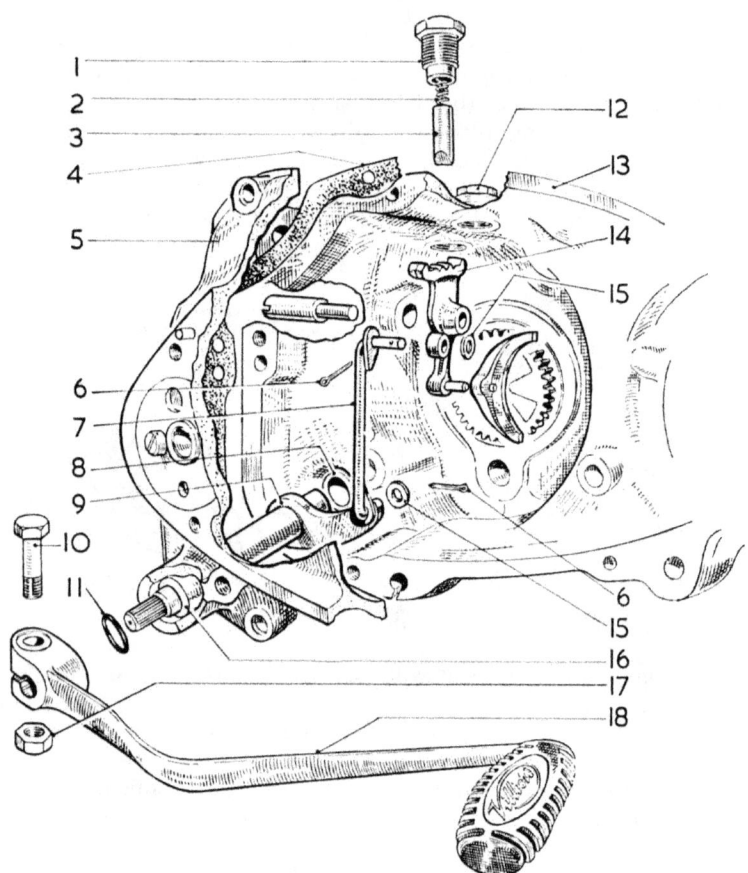

FIG. 46. MARK 6F GEAR-CHANGE MECHANISM

1. Plunger box
2. Plunger spring
3. Plunger
4. Joint washer
5. Clutch case
6. Split pin
7. Link rod assembly
8. Gearcase bush
9. Pedal shaft assembly
10. Bolt for kick-starter
11. Sealing washer
12. Gearcase plug
13. Gearcase
14. Gear selector lever
15. Washer for link rod
16. Clutchcase bush
17. Nut for kick-starter bolt
18. Gear-change lever

control lever and the other half-way down between the lever and the gearbox, but it is important to see that the screw at the gear control lever is kept quite tight otherwise the lever will become loose.

The latest design of gear-change mechanism for four-speed gearboxes is shown in Fig. 47.

Clutch and Primary Drive Adjustment (Engines Mark 9E, 2L, 31C). Little attention beyond that of maintaining adequate lubrication, is necessary for the chain which runs from the engine to the clutch: it runs in an

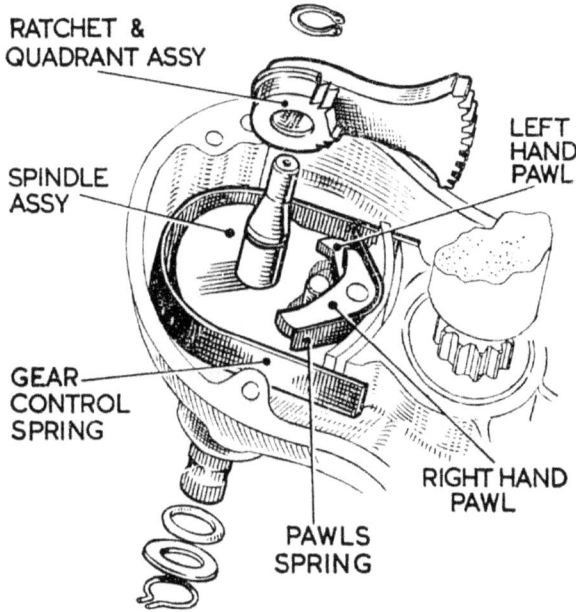

FIG. 47. GEAR-CHANGE MECHANISM (NEW PATTERN)

oil bath. It is important, however, to adjust the clearance of the push-rod as regularly as may be found necessary, in order to avoid clutch slip. Clearance has to be maintained between the end of the push-rod, which is located in the hollow gearbox main shaft, and the clutch lever, which is fitted to the gearbox end cover. A slotted adjuster provides for this and access to it can be gained via a hole in the right-hand outer casing or fan casing. A screwdriver is used for the adjustment.

For those engines with a covered clutch lever (Fig. 48) the adjuster on the clutch control cable should be slackened off and then the adjusting screw and the casing should be moved by use of the screwdriver until there is $\frac{1}{8}$ in. free play between the clutch lever end and the right-hand cover. Slack in the control cable is now taken up, so that there is $\frac{1}{16}$ in.

free movement of the lever before the clutch spring starts to be depressed. Lastly, the cable adjuster lock-nut is tightened, but when doing this make certain that there is no end pressure at all on the push-rod while the clutch is engaged. The corks, although running in oil, become worn in time and

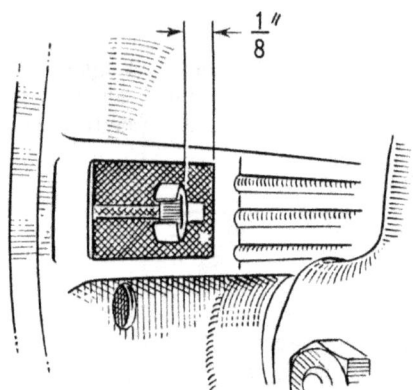

Fig. 48. Showing the Free Play Necessary between the Covered Clutch Lever End and Right-hand Cover (Marks 9E, 2L, 31C)

one should be always on the look out for slight slipping, so that the push-rod adjustment can be made in good time.

Engines which have an exposed clutch lever (*see* Fig. 49) are adjusted in more or less the same way. The adjuster on the control cable is slackened

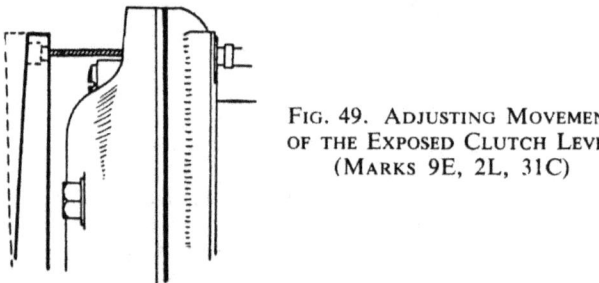

Fig. 49. Adjusting Movement of the Exposed Clutch Lever (Marks 9E, 2L, 31C)

off and a screwdriver placed in the slot of the clutch lever adjusting screw which is then moved so that the clutch lever is in the position shown in the sketch. All one has to do now is to take up any slack in the cable so that there is $\frac{1}{16}$ in. movement of the clutch lever before it starts to depress the clutch spring, after which the cable adjuster lock-nut is tightened up, making sure that there is no end pressure on the push-rod while the clutch is engaged.

ADJUSTING AND OVERHAULING

Apart from the foregoing, the clutch can only remain efficient if the push-rod has an effective length which will maintain adequate operation. This adjustment is quite easily made by altering the adjuster which will be found in the centre of the clutch cap cut (*see* Fig. 50). The clutch lever is best removed so that one can see the distance to which the push-rod protrudes through the gearbox end cover, which should be $\frac{5}{16}$ in. After the necessary adjustment has been made one must see that the lock-nut is fully tightened, otherwise it will shake loose and upset the adjustment.

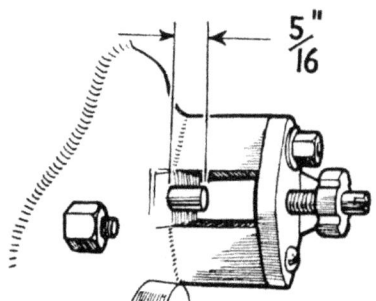

FIG. 50. ADJUSTMENT OF THE CLUTCH PUSH-ROD
(MARKS 9E, 2L, 31C)

It is as well to check up on the push-rod setting when the oil is changed in the crankcase because then the adjusting screw is more readily accessible.

Clutch and Primary Drive Adjustments (Marks 2T and 3T). Clutch adjustment for these engines is carried out in the same manner as for the engine dealt with in the foregoing paragraph, except that the adjuster screw should be moved until there is $\frac{1}{16}$ in. movement between the right-hand cover and the bottom end of the clutch lever. The clutch control cable adjuster should then be positioned to allow the inner cable to move freely over at least $\frac{1}{8}$ in. The adjustment of the clutch push-rod is carried out in the same manner as already described.

The drive from the engine to the multi-plate clutch is by a $\frac{3}{8}$ in. pitch pre-stretched roller chain running in an oil-bath chain case; no attention is necessary beyond lubrication and occasionally adjusting the push-rod and lever.

Decarbonizing. Decarbonizing means the removal of the carbon which is formed inside the engine by the combustion of the petroil-air mixture. When this layer of carbon becomes excessive certain faults will occur, such as preignition, harsh running, overheating, reduction of power, and increased fuel consumption.

A rider in tune with his machine will appreciate when the engine seems to lose power or the acceleration becomes poor. In some cases such as with the Marks 9E, 31C, and 2L engines, it is recommended that the engines be decarbonized every 2,000 miles and in the case of the Mark 4F and 2T engines, every 5,000 miles, but a good deal depends upon the manner in which the engine is treated. It is better to err on the more frequent side.

Before decarbonizing can be attempted, the sparking plug should be removed, the petrol pipe and carburettor disconnected and the exhaust pipe and silencer removed.

It is then possible to remove the cylinder-head fixing-bolts after which the head can be lifted away from the barrel. It is as well to have ready a new gasket for fitting between the cylinder barrel and head, even though the existing gasket appears to be undamaged.

The areas which attract carbon and which must be carefully cleaned are the top of the piston, the cylinder head, and all round and just inside the ports, as well as the exhaust pipe and silencer.

If the engines are fitted with a cowling this will, of course, have to be removed in order that the cylinder head can be taken off.

Using a soft copper scraper, remove all the carbon from the cylinder head first and if the fins are dirty, then the whole lot can be cleaned with a brush and paraffin.

Next, bring the piston to the top of its stroke and remove the carbon from the top face. Then rotate the engine to bring the piston to the bottom so that the edges of the ports and the exhaust stub and other parts can be cleaned both from the inside and the outside. Ports which have been cleaned should be stuffed with pieces of soft cloth to prevent loose pieces of carbon or even a nut or washer from falling in.

The exhaust pipe and silencer can best be cleaned by using a long-handled screwdriver.

Cylinder Removal. (Refer to Figs. 51, 52, 53 and 54.) It is rarely necessary to examine the rings, gudgeon pin and so on under 10,000 miles, but the amateur should find no great difficulty in doing this himself. In order to take the cylinder off safely, the piston should be at the bottom of its stroke.

The cylinder should be pulled straight off and not twisted or the piston rings may be broken if their ends are caught up in the ports.

In the engines Mark 2T and 3T, just below the inlet pipe is the head of the crankcase pinch bolt which must not be touched.

The gudgeon-pin is held in position by spring circlips and one should be taken out by using a pair of thin-nosed pliers after which the gudgeon-pin can be pushed out of its small-end bush which will release the piston.

If the carbon deposits are heavy, it may not be possible to push the gudgeon-pin out by hand in which case both circlips will have to be removed and a band extractor used. Most pistons are marked "front" and they should always be fitted the same way round as when removed. With twin-cylinder engines it is important to see that the pistons do not get changed over from one cylinder to the other.

It will probably be found that carbon has formed in the piston-ring grooves and to make a good job of the cleaning, the rings will have to be sprung off. Here again, the particular groove from which a ring came must be noted. Behind the lower ring an "expander" ring, which is fitted to obviate piston slap when the engine is cold, usually will be found. Because of the heat in the area where this ring is situated, it is likely to lose its springiness and it is advisable when decarbonizing to renew it.

In order to remove and replace the rings without damage three pieces of thin brass strip can be spaced equally around the piston so that the rings can be slid off.

To free the grooves of carbon probably the best possible method is to use the end of a broken piston ring.

If the piston rings are in good order, they must obviously be in contact all round the cylinder bore; this is indicated by the bright surface of the rings. The gap between the ends of the rings when fitted in the cylinder, should not exceed 0·03 in. Should the gap be excessive new rings should be fitted. The gap can be checked by putting the ring in the cylinder and pushing it up with the piston skirt, the gap then being checked with a feeler gauge.

It is always as well to check the gap of new rings before the piston is fitted. When the ring is in the cylinder bore, the gap between the ring ends should be a minimum of 0·007 in. and maximum of 0·011 in.

If there is a ridge around the top of the bore, it would be as well to get your local garage to check on the degree of wear. If the bore is 0·008 in. or more larger than the original bore, it would be advisable to send the cylinder to the Villiers works for reboring, plus the fitting of an oversize piston with rings.

If, on the other hand, the cylinder bore does not appear to be badly worn, then after decarbonizing, the engine can be reassembled. It is better to provide new washers where necessary rather than to use the old ones. The fitting of the cylinder over the piston needs to be done with care to avoid breaking the rings. The surface of the piston and the cylinder bore should be smeared with clean engine oil so that the barrel will slide down easily over the piston rings. When doing this care must be taken not to twist the cylinder in any way. The rings should be gently eased into position, taking particular note that the ends are properly fitted on the locating pegs as the cylinder barrel comes down over them. The nuts or bolts securing the cylinder head and the nuts on the cylinder-base studs should be tightened carefully in diagonal rotation in order to avoid any possibility of distortion.

Then follows the fitting of the exhaust pipe and silencer and the final tightening of the carburettor nuts.

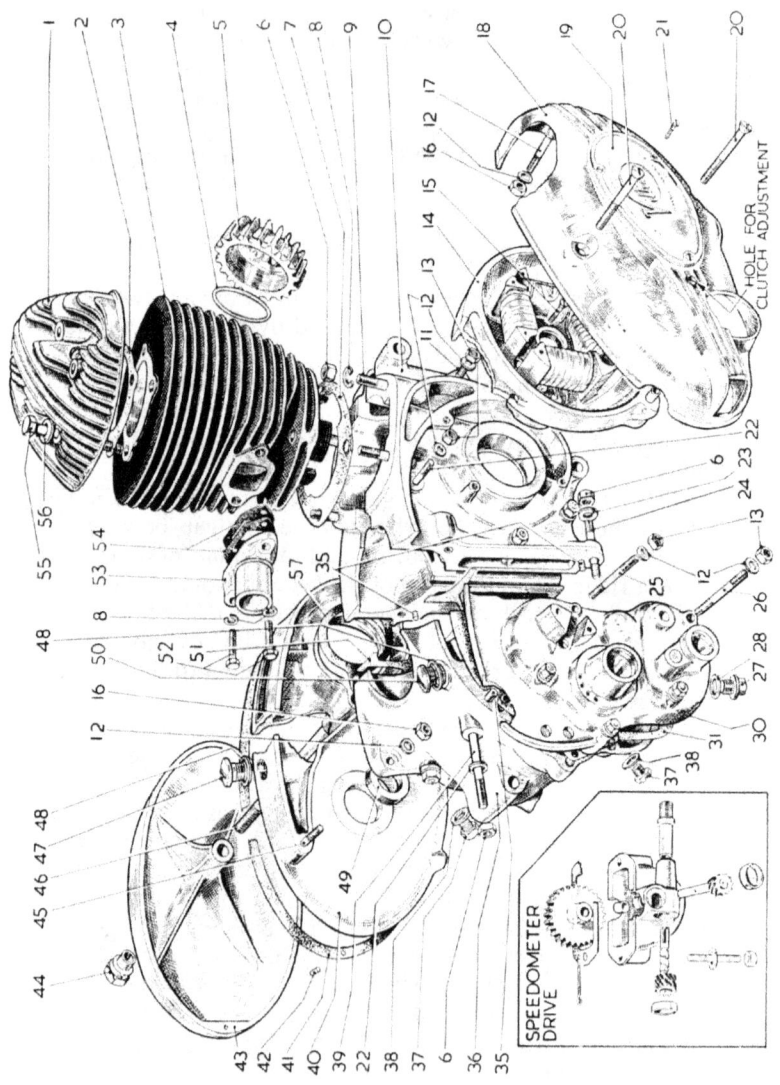

FIG. 51. ENGINE DETAILS, MARK 9E (ALSO 2L AND 31C)

1. Cylinder head
2. Cylinder-head joint washer
3. Cylinder (9E)
4. Exhaust nut washer
5. Exhaust nut
7. Cylinder-base washer
9. Cylinder-base stud
10. Crankcase
11. Crankcase stud
14. Armature plate assembly
16. Nut for cover stud
18. Right-hand cover four-speed gearbox
19. Contact-breaker cover
27. Gearbox drain plug
31. Gearbox end-cover joint washer
35. Crankcase and gearbox dowels
36. Gearbox casing
37. Chaincase and gearbox oil-level plug
40. Inner chaincase
41. Chaincase joint washer
42. Chaincase dowel
43. Outer chaincase
47. Chaincase filler plug
48. Chaincase filler plug and dipstick washer
49. Chaincase gland plate
50. Gearbox oil-level dipstick
51. Joint washer
52. Inlet manifold fixing-screw
53. Inlet manifold
54. Inlet manifold washer
55. Cylinder head bolt
57. Joint washer for inner chaincase to crankcase

(Inset shows speedometer drive assembly)
In this illustration (*see* opposite page) major items only are listed

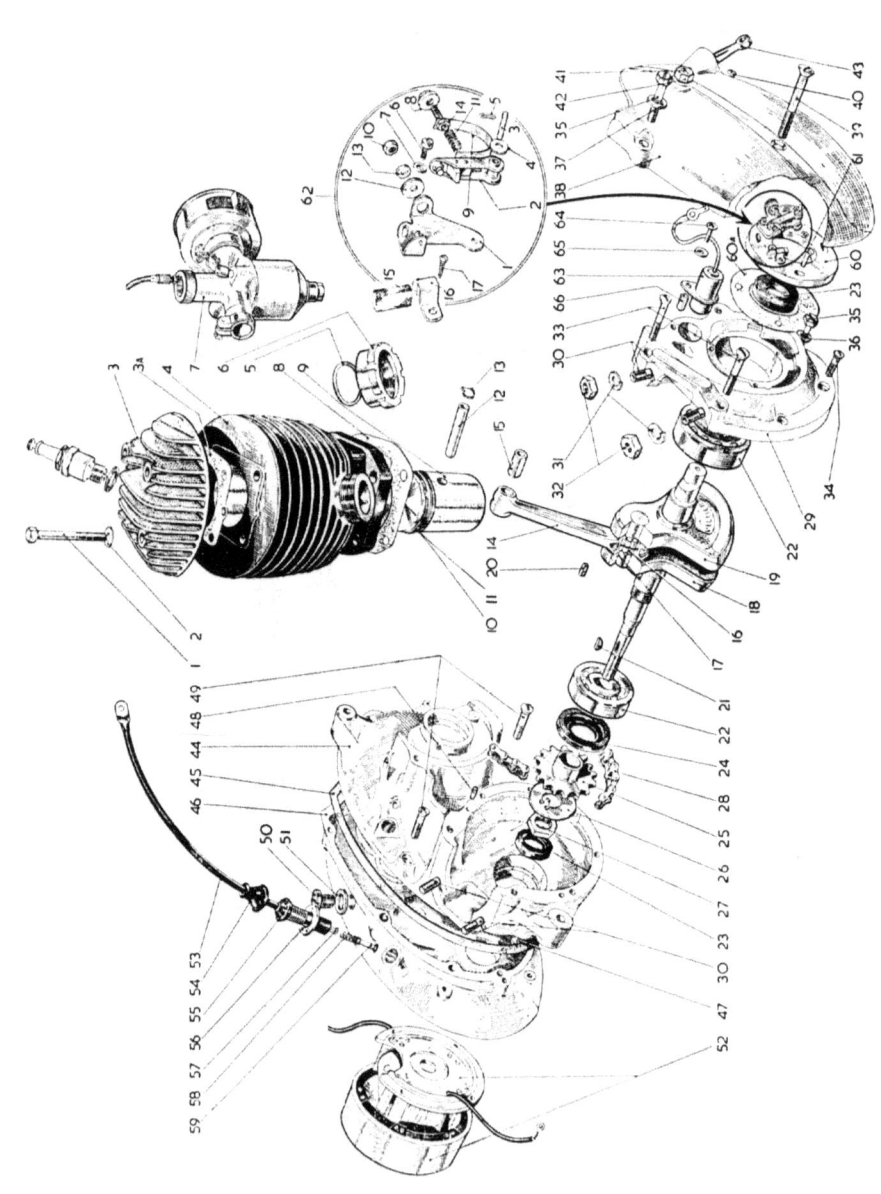

FIG. 52. ENGINE AND CONTACT-BREAKER DETAILS
MARKS 4F AND 6F

1. Cylinder-head bolt
2. Cylinder head
3a. Cylinder-head gasket
4. Cylinder
5. Exhaust nut washer
6. Exhaust nut
7. Carburettor
8. Cylinder-base gasket
9. Piston
10. Piston ring
11. Expander ring
12. Gudgeon pin
13. Circlip
14. Connecting rod
15. Small-end bush
16. Rollers for crankpin
17. Crankpin
18. Right-hand drive shaft
19. Left-hand drive shaft
20. Engine sprocket key
21. Flywheel key
22. Ball bearing
23. Oil Seal
24. Gaco oil seal
25. Engine sprocket
26. Lock washer
28. Primary chain

29. Crankcase door
30. Cylinder base studs
35. Crankcase drain plug and clutch bridge bolt
38. Left-hand cover
41. Clutch lever adjusting screw
43. Clutch lever
44. Gear case
45. Clutch case gasket
46. Clutch case
47. Dowels in gear case
48. Dowels in gear case for crankcase door
50. Oil filler plug
52. Magneto assembly
53. High-tension lead
54. Rubber cover
55. High-tension terminal holder
56. Felt washer
57 and 58. Brass terminal screw and spring
59. Terminal screw pad
60. Contact-breaker adaptor
60a. Gasket for adaptor
62. Contact-breaker assembly
63. Condenser
66. Distance piece

Contact-breaker Assembly (62)

1. Contact-breaker point bracket
2. Rocker arm assembly
3. Pivot pin
4. Washer
5. Split pin
6. Point bracket screw
7. Brass washer
8. Low-tension terminal bush
9. Connecting strip
10. Nut
11. Spring
12. Insulating washer
13. Washer
14. Low-tension terminal screw
15. Oil pad
16. Oil-pad clip
17. Screw for clip and seal retaining washer

In this illustration (*see opposite page*) major parts only are identified

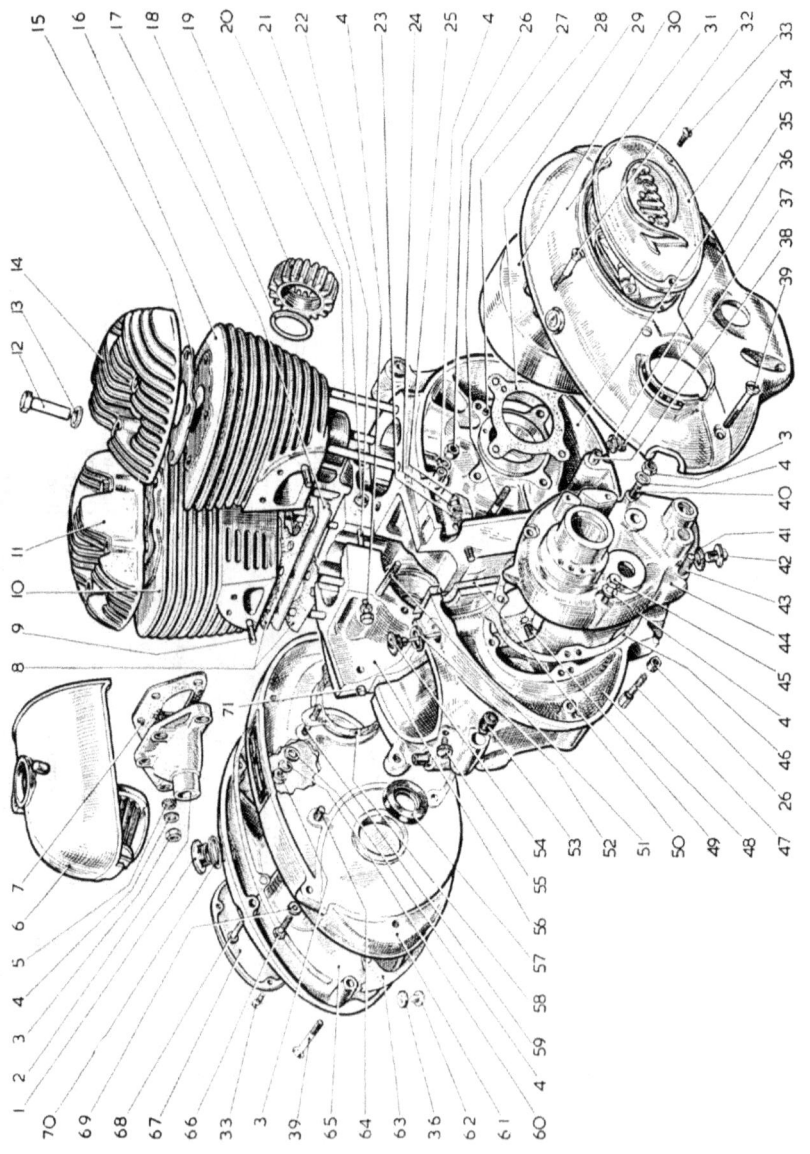

FIG. 53. ENGINE DETAILS OF THE MARKS 2T AND 3T UNITS

1. Chaincase filler cap
2. Inlet pipe
6. Carburettor and air filter
7. Inlet pipe joint washer
8. Cylinder-base-joint washer
10. Left-hand cylinder
11. Left-hand cylinder head
14. Right-hand cylinder head
15. Cylinder-head joint washer
16. Right-hand cylinder
17. Cylinder joint plate
18. Exhaust pipe nut washer
19. Exhaust pipe nut
21. Pinch bolt trunnion
22. Left-hand crankcase pinch bolt
25. Cable clip
28. Armature-plate dowel
29. Armature-plate joint washer
30. Magneto assembly
31. Right-hand cover
34. Contact-breaker cover
35. Right-hand crankcase
37. Drain screw
42. Gearbox drain plug
44. Gearbox end-cover
46. Gearbox end-cover joint washer
47. Clutch cable adjuster
48. Gearbox shell
50. Gearbox crankcase joint washer
51. Crankcase aligning stud
52. Dipstick washer
53. Crankcase mounting lug bush
54. Gearbox dipstick
56. Left-hand crankcase
57. Chaincase oil-seal
58. Crankcase-chaincase joint washer
61. Crankcase (rear half)
62. Chaincase oil-level screw
63. Chaincase joint washer
64. Screw
65. Crankcase (front half)
66. Screw
67. Left-hand nameplate cover
71. Gearbox dowel

In this illustration (*see* opposite page) major parts only are identified

In this illustration major items only are listed

2. Cover fan and gauze
3. Fan-hub assembly
4. Chaincase filter plug
8. Cowl
9. Cylinder
13. Cylinder head
18. Cowl bottom and outer chain-case
32. Right-hand cover
38. Gearbox end cover
45 and 46. Drive shafts
52. Gear-change lever

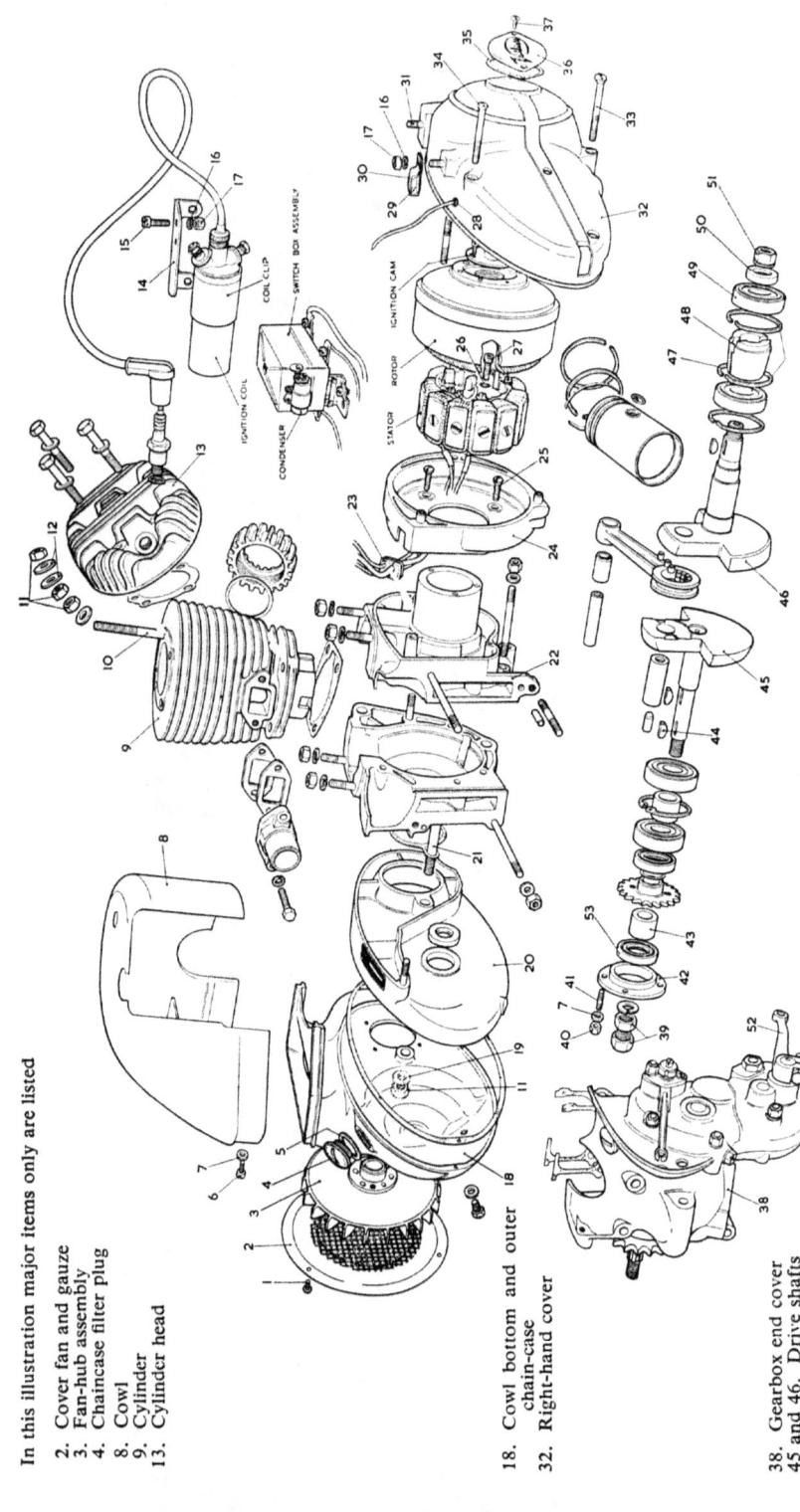

Fig. 54. The Latest Type Cowled Engine with Self-Starter

ADJUSTING AND OVERHAULING 81

Dismantling and Major Overhauls. Few amateurs have the expert knowledge or equipment or indeed the desire to effect a major repair.

If any serious fault has developed, it is advisable to contact the local Norton–Villiers agent or to return the engine complete to the Norton–Villiers Service Department.

If it appears that a complete major overhaul is called for, it is probably better to send the engine, complete with its carburettor and magneto, through your agent, or direct to the works and obtain a fully reconditioned part-exchange engine, which carries the same guarantee as a new unit.

With any repair, it is advisable to get an estimate before the repair is proceeded with. On the other hand, an estimate cannot be prepared until the engine has been taken down to see what new parts will be required. If the estimate is not accepted, there will probably be a labour charge for dismantling and reassembling.

If a complete overhaul is not called for, the existing cylinder can be rebored, and a suitable oversize piston fitted, or a reconditioned crankshaft assembly can be provided in exchange for the original assembly.

The same excellent service can be arranged for a reconditioned magneto in part-exchange. The recorking of a clutch can also be carried out on a similar exchange plan. It will probably be more convenient to arrange the exchange through your local Villiers Agent.

Tracing Troubles. If an engine ceases to function as it should, there are three main points to be checked. First of all, see that the correct quantity of petroil and air can enter the engine; secondly, that the mixture can be fired at the right time by a good spark from the plug; thirdly, that the engine itself is in good fettle, so that there are no air leaks at any of the joints, and that there is good compression in both the cylinder and crankcase.

It is much better to carry through an orderly investigation in proper sequence than to make haphazard tests. In order to diagnose the trouble as easily as possible the procedure given in the fault-finding chart on pages 90–2 should be followed.

THE SPARKING PLUGS

Plug Gap. The gap at the points of the sparking plug should be from 0·018 in. to 0·025 in. for all engines except Marks 33A and 34A, which should be 0·018 in. to 0·022 in. Check and if necessary adjust the *earth* electrode(s) with a plug re-gapping tool having feeler gauges.

Diagnosing Troubles. When checking the plug point gap, examine the condition of the plug as this is one of the best indications as to whether the engine is running under the best conditions or not (*see* Fig. 55).

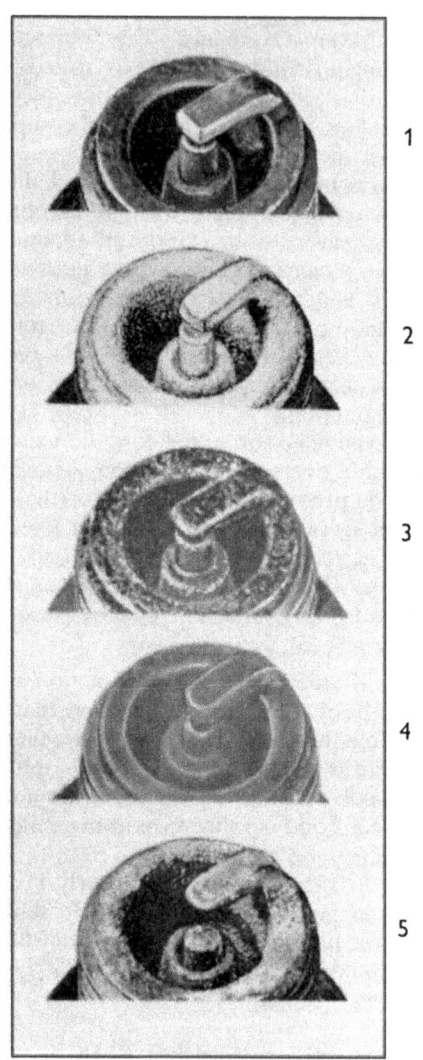

FIG. 55. SPARKING PLUG TROUBLE-DIAGNOSIS

1. Correct type of plug under satisfactory conditions with light flaky deposit on rim and horizontal electrode.
2. Use of wrong type of plug showing excessive bleached deposits, the result of running too hot; carburation may be faulty giving too weak mixture or engine needs decarbonizing.
3. Engine running too cool so that plug has not reached its self-cleaning temperature; change to more suitable type of plug.
4. A heavily sooted plug indicating the use of a too rich mixture.
5. A plug which is worn out and cannot be made serviceable by cleaning or adjustment.

(*Courtesy of Lodge Plugs Ltd.*)

SUITABLE SPARKING PLUGS FOR VILLIERS ENGINES

Villiers Engine (c.c.)		Champion	K.L.G.	Bosch	Lodge	A.C. Delco
Mk. 3K	(50)	L-81 or L-5	—	W95T1	—	44FA or M44F
Mk. 7	(75)	—	F20	W95T1	BN	—
Mk. 7/1	(75)	—	F50	W145T1	CN	44FA or M45F
Junior	(98)	L-90 or L-10	F50	W225T1	CN	C85H
Junior de Luxe	(98)	7 Com. L	ML30	W240T1	CB3	44FA or M44F
Mks. 1F, 2F, 4F, 6F	(98)	L-86 or L-7	F75	W225T1	HN	C86H
Midget	(98)	8 Com.	—	—	—	C83H
Mks. 8D, 9D	(122)	L-86 or L-7	M60	M175T1	HV	44FA or M44F
Mks. 10D, 12D, 13D	(127)	L-86 or L-7	F75	W225T1	HN	44FA or M44F
Mk. 11D	(122)	L-81 or L-5	F75	W225T1	HN	C86H
Mk. 8C	(147)	8 Com.	M50	—	CV	—
29C Comp. Fan-Cooled 30C	(147)	L-81 or L-5	F75	W225T1	HN	44FA or M44F
Mk. 30C	(147)	L-86 or L-7	F75	W225T1	HN	44FA or M44F
Mks. 12C, 15C	(148)	7 Com. L	ML30	—	CB3	C85H
Mk. 31C	(148)	L-81 or L-5	F80	W225T1	2HN	42FA or M42F
Sports	(172)	—	ML30	W240T1	CB3	—
Mks. 2L, 3L	(173)	L-81 or L-5	F80	—	2HN	42FA or M42F
Mks. 1E, 2E, 3E	(197)	7 Com. L	—	—	—	C85H
Mk. 5E	(197)	K9	—	—	—	C82
Mks. 6E, 7E, 8E, 9E, 10E, 11E, 35F, 45F	(197)	L-81 or L-5	F80	W240T1	2HN	42FA or M42F

SUITABLE SPARKING PLUGS (CONTD.)

Villiers Engine (c.c.)		Champion	K.L.G.	Bosch	Lodge	A.C. Delco
Super Sports 9E	(197)	7 Com. L	F80	W240T1	2HN	C85H
Mk. 1H	(225)	L-81 or L-5	F80	W240T1	2HN	42FA or M42F
Mk. 2H	(246)	L-86 or L-7	F80	W240T1	2HN	42FA or M42F
Mks. 31A/45, 31A/3S, 32A	(246)	L-81 or L-5	F80	W240T1	2HN	42FA or M42F
Mks. 33A, 34A, 35A, 37A	(246)	L-81 or L-5	FE80	W240T2	2HLN or RL49	43XL
36A Parkinson	(246)	L-57R	—	—	RL49	—
Starmaker Trials	(247)	L-86	—	W175T1	RL49	—
Starmaker Scrambles	(247)	N-57R	—	W175T1	RL49	—
Starmaker Racing	(247)	N-54R	—	W175T1	RL49	—
2T twin	(249)	L-86 or L-7	F80	W240T1	2HN	42FA or M42F
14A, 17A, 18A	(249)	7 Com. L	ML30	W240T1	CB3	C85H
4T twin	(250)	L-81 or L-5	F80	W240T1	2HN	42FA or M42F
3T and 4T twin	(324)	L-81 or L-5	F80	W240T1	2HN	42FA or M42F
14B, 27B	(346)	7 Com. L	ML30	W240T1	CB3	C85H
28B	(353)	L-81 or L-5	F80	W240T1	2HN	42FA or M42F

CLEANING PLUGS. Most of the sparking plugs specified in the foregoing 2-page chart are of the *non-detachable* type, but many are of the *detachable* type. Whatever type of plug your Villiers engine has, the quickest and best method of cleaning it is to take it to your nearest garage equipped with a plug service unit. Within a few minutes your plug(s) can be cleaned by sand-blasting of all deposits, thoroughly washed, subjected to a high-pressure air line and finally tested for efficient sparking on the service unit.

If your plug is of the *detachable* type (e.g. K.L.G.) you can, if you wish, dismantle the plug with a box-spanner, clean its insulation with a cloth soaked in petrol or paraffin and remove its deposits with fine glass-paper. Deposits from all metal parts should be scraped off with a small pocket-knife or a wire brush. When dismantling or assembling a detachable type plug be most careful not to over-tighten its gland nut. The electrode points should be cleaned and polished with some fine glass-paper or the fine file of a plug re-gapping tool. Check that the gap (*see* page 81) is correct *after* cleaning.

8 The Siba Dynastart

THIS dual-purpose component performs the duties not only of a self-starter from a 12-volt battery, but also of a flywheel magneto. When a starter button is pushed, a solenoid is operated which brings the Dynastart into use as a series motor thus rotating the engine. Conversely, the Dynastart is then driven by the engine and the current so generated is used for ignition, for battery charging and for lighting.

As the engine increases its speed so does the voltage increase up to a maximum of 12 volts when the cut-out switch closes and the battery begins to be charged. The voltage is held by an automatic control and as current is used so the voltage drops in conformity with the output. The optimum charging rate is reached at speeds between 1,200 and 1,500 r.p.m. and will carry a regular load of 90 watts.

This self-starter can be fitted to the following Villiers engines: Marks 9E/3S, 9E/4S, 9E/4SF, 2L/3SF, 2L/4SF, 31C/3SF, 31C/4SF, 2T/S, 2T/SF, and 3T/SF.

The unit (see Fig. 56) is made up of a 12-pole stator (six for the shunt windings and six for the starter windings), a bell-type armature, contact-breaker, an ignition coil, voltage regulator, condenser, cut-out and starter solenoid.

Routine Overhauling. The importance of the electric starter is such that it is as well to know how to carry out normal and simple maintenance.

ARMATURE (ROTOR). Perhaps the greatest need is to keep the brushes and commutator clean and it is recommended that at periods not exceeding 5,000 miles the armature should be removed and the brushes thoroughly cleaned. The trouble lies in the accumulation of carbon dust and after long periods of use possible wear of the brushes.

The engine cover should be removed first and also the timing cam and the centre hexagon nut, but when effecting an overhaul, great care must be taken not to damage the armature windings. The dust should be removed with a soft brush. It is as well to have handy a new carbon brush from which one can gauge the degree of wear which has taken place in the brushes in use.

CONTACT-BREAKER. This assembly is housed in the cover and it can be easily removed by taking out the screws securing it. The gap should be kept at 0·020 in, to 0·022 in., with the piston at top-dead-centre. It is

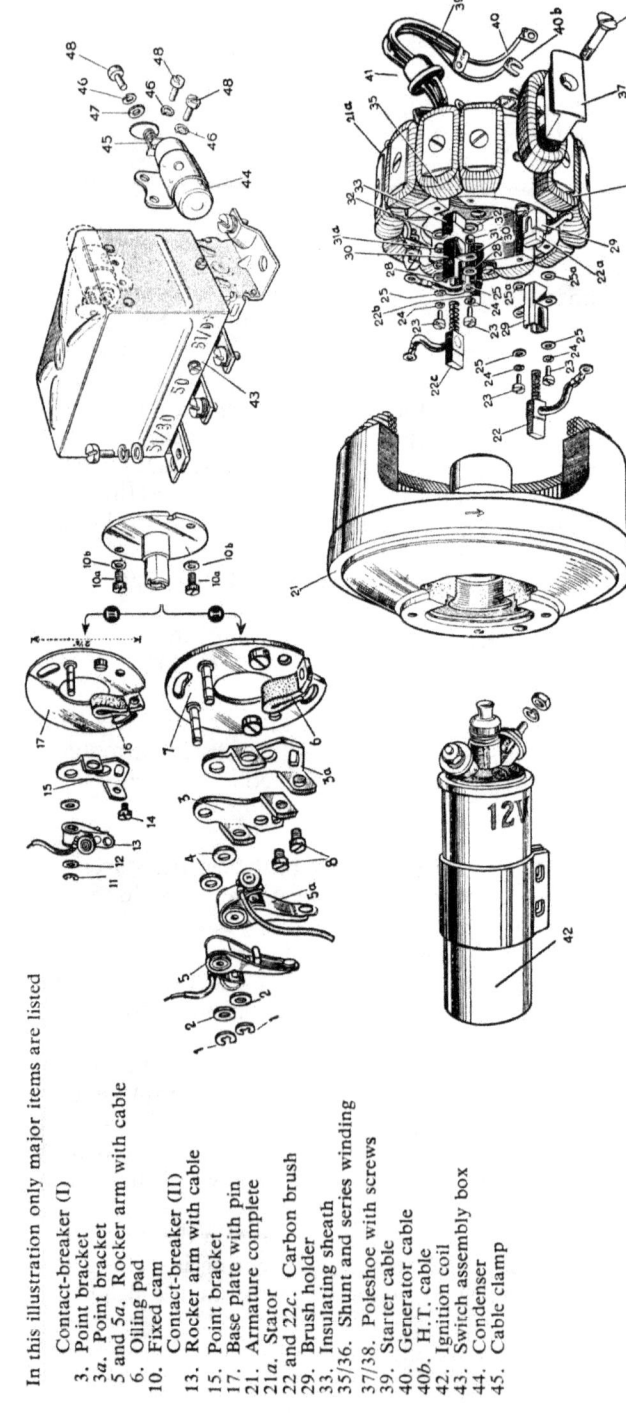

In this illustration only major items are listed

    Contact-breaker (I)
 3. Point bracket
 3a. Point bracket
 5 and 5a. Rocker arm with cable
 6. Oiling pad
10. Fixed cam
13. Contact-breaker (II)
    Rocker arm with cable
15. Point bracket
17. Base plate with pin
21. Armature complete
21a. Stator
22 and 22c. Carbon brush
29. Brush holder
33. Insulating sheath
35/36. Shunt and series winding
37/38. Poleshoe with screws
39. Starter cable
40. Generator cable
40b. H.T. cable
42. Ignition coil
43. Switch assembly box
44. Condenser
45. Cable clamp

Fig. 56. Exploded View of the SIBA Dynastart Uni-directional Unit

important to keep the breaker points clean and properly adjusted and one should refer to pages 19–20 for details.

Unless replacements are called for it will not be necessary to remove the assembly. If the assembly base plate has to be removed then of course, the ignition must be retimed. The ignition is retarded if the assembly is turned clockwise and vice versa. It is important especially with twin-cylinder engines to see that the rocker-arm heel is properly bedded down to the cam before the ignition is timed, otherwise wrong adjustment will be made.

THE STATOR. It is rarely necessary to remove the stator and the inner housing. If it is thought desirable then the battery and cables will have to be disconnected from the switch assembly box. It will be found that three socket-headed screws secure the stator to the crankcase spigot, and the inner housing to the crankcase by four screws. When these are removed the stator and the inner housing are easily lifted away from the crankcase spigot, but care must be taken not to damage the oil-seal in the stator.

If the switch assembly in its sealed box has developed a defect, then it should be returned for repair to the manufacturers. The removal of the cover automatically invalidates the guarantee.

REASSEMBLY. There are certain details which are important when reassembling the unit.

A jointing compound must be used to ensure perfect sealing of the faces of the stator and crankcase spigot. Before fitting the stator and the housing to the crankcase spigot, the crankcase oil-seal must be in its proper position and the stator, inner housing and cables correctly located.

It is most important to use the jointing compound in the manner indicated by the manufacturers because if a complete seal is not made, oil will find its way on to the brush gear and commutator. Not only will the starter then fail to operate but the commutator may be severely damaged.

In order to avoid serious trouble from loosening of any parts, the screws which hold the stator inner housing to the crankcase must be locked by punching metal into the screw slot and it is also important that the shake-proof washers are replaced on the three fixing screws. The brushes must lie properly in their holders so that they are quite free, with the pigtail connexions lying against the stator windings.

Just prior to the armature being fitted to the shaft, the drive shaft key must be accurately positioned. When tightening the centre nut, care must be taken not to damage the armature. All tapers must be clean and to make certain that the armature does not foul the stator it should be rotated by hand after tightening.

And lastly, be sure that the cables are connected up correctly as shown in the wiring diagram Fig. 57.

Fault Finding. Nothing is more annoying than a starter which fails to operate. If the battery is known to be in good condition and fully charged

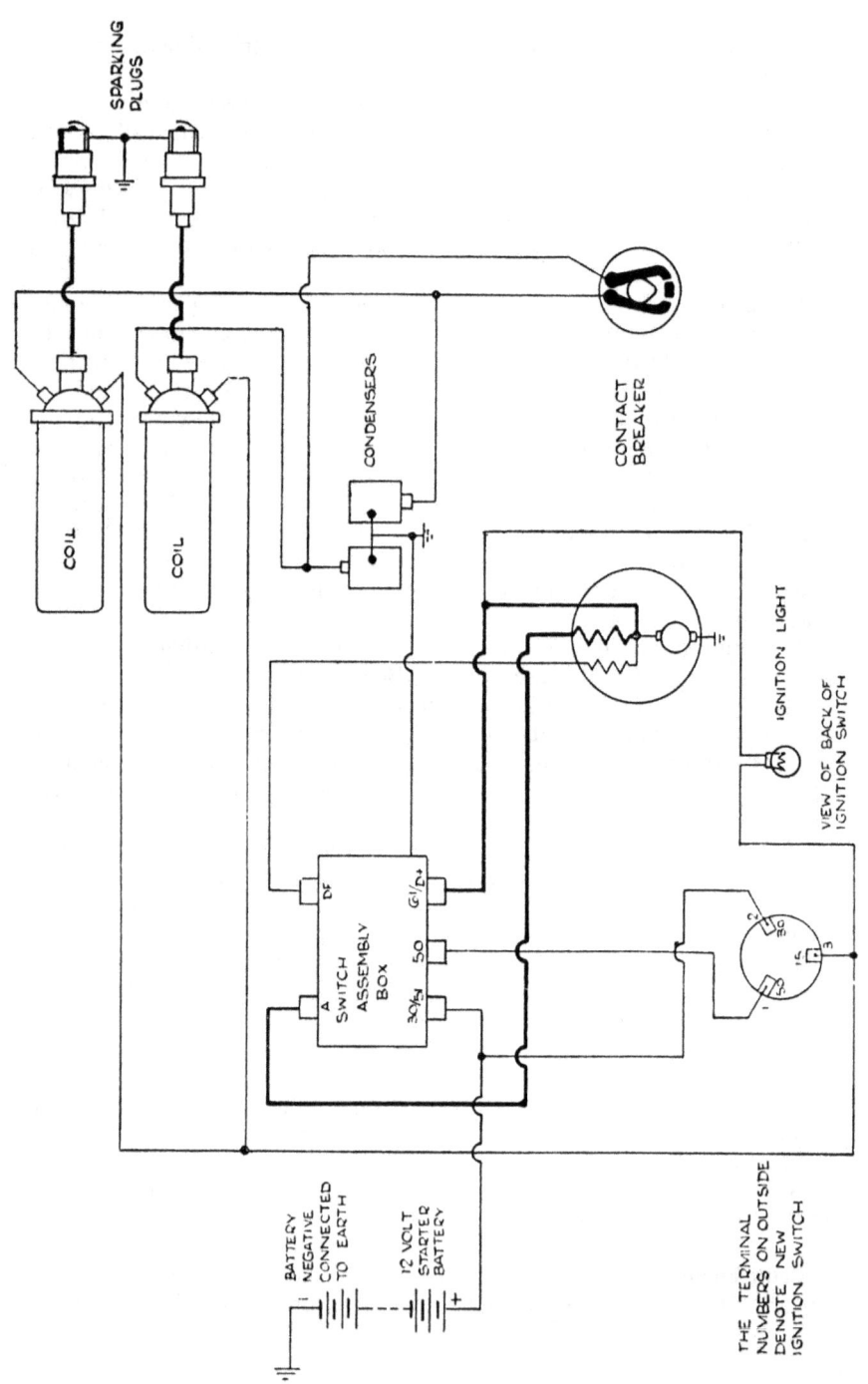

THE SIBA DYNASTART

and yet the starter does not work, do not keep on pressing the starter button or turning the ignition key. If there is no quick response then the fault must be found and rectified to prevent serious damage.

If the starter refuses to function then the battery may be flat or the electrolite level may have been allowed to drop excessively. Alternatively, battery connexions may be loose, or severely corroded.

If when the battery is connected excessive sparking takes place, it may indicate a short circuit in the wiring and it would be advisable to take it to a garage where the trouble could be quickly spotted.

In rare cases the solenoid may fail, possibly due to a fault in the wiring or, in rare instances, to some trouble in the switch assembly box.

Faults which may well develop if the unit itself if not kept in proper condition by regular maintenance may be, excessive wear on the carbon brushes, or a brush which has become jammed in its holder; the stator may also foul the armature due to incorrect reassembly, or there may be oil on the commutator. If serious trouble develops due to faults in the armature and stator then the unit should be returned to the manufacturer.

Starter Works—Engine Fails. Sometimes whilst the starter is fully capable of turning the engine over there may be no sign of life from the engine. It is as well to check up to see whether there is a spark at the plug first. The contact-breaker assembly should be checked over to see that the arm is moving freely and that the points are clean and the gap correct. In a few cases the trouble may be due to a defective ignition coil or condenser; if this is so a new component should be fitted.

If the ignition warning lamp does not light when the ignition is switched on, the battery may be flat, or the bulb may have fused, or there may be a faulty connexion. Rarely the timing cam may be at fault; if it is it should be renewed.

If the ignition warning lamp does not go out when the engine revolutions exceed 1,300 r.p.m. on a machine which has been used for some time then there may be some trouble in the wiring. Occasionally, the cut-out or the regulator develops a fault; then the switch assembly box should be replaced.

In conjunction with these possible faults one should refer also to the fault-finding chart on page 90. Details of the Dynastart are given in Fig. 56 in which only the major items have been identified in the key.

ENGINE FAULT-FINDING CHART

- Engine will not start
  - Carburettor floods on depressing needle
    - Spark at plug
      - Controls sticking
      - Air leakage
      - Spark too weak to fire under compression
      - Short in plug, terminal or H.T. lead
      - Too rich mixture
      - Use of strangler when hot
      - Choked with carbon
      - Petrol in crankcase
      - Air leaks
    - No spark at plug
      - Spark at H.T. lead
        - Faulty plug
        - Sooted plug points
        - Weak spark
        - Short circuit
      - No spark at H.T. lead
        - Magneto contact-breaker arm free
          - Breaker arm sticking
          - Dirty contact points
          - Faulty contact points
          - Failure in magneto insulation
          - Contact at various points broken
          - Faulty ignition coil
          - Faulty condenser
  - No petrol at carburettor
    - Petrol tap open
      - Pipe clear
        - Petrol tap closed
        - Choked pipe, filter blocked
        - Air lock in pipe
        - Air vent to tank blocked
        - No petrol in tank

ENGINE FAULT-FINDING CHART

- Engine runs imperfectly
  - Lacks power
    - Constantly
      - Controls out of order
      - Controls in order
        - Poor compression
          - Incorrect mixture
          - Choked with carbon
          - Cylinder head bolts loose
          - Brakes binding
          - Air cleaner choked
          - Worn piston rings or cylinder
          - Choked silencer
          - Leakage in crankcase
          - Ignition incorrectly set
          - Gear too high
          - Wrong carburettor setting
          - Obstruction in petrol pipe
          - Dirty exhaust port
          - Partial obstruction of fuel supply
          - Bad plug, carbon deposit
    - at intervals
      - Overheating
      - Sooted plug
      - Dirty contact-breaker, breaker points too close
      - Occasional short in H.T. lead
      - Mixture too weak
      - Water in petrol
      - Starved carburettor
      - Air vent to petrol tank blocked
  - Engine knocks
    - Too high a gear
    - Engine carbonized
    - Choked silencer
    - Ignition too far advanced
    - Mixture too weak
    - Unsuitable type of sparking plug
  - Misses fire
    - Spark irregular
    - Spark regular
  - Fails on hills
    - Correct gear ratio
      - Engine clean
  - Fails, and after a momentary rest will re-start quite well
  - Four or eight strokes
    - Too rich mixture
    - Air strangler closed
    - Air filter choked
    - Carburettor flooded or dirty

ENGINE FAULT-FINDING CHART

- Engine stops
  - Petrol
    - Spark at plug points
      - Compression
        - Carburetor working
          - No petrol, or tap turned off
          - Controls not working
          - Overheating—pre-ignition
          - Insufficient lubrication
          - Air leakage
        - Carburetor not working
          - Choked jet or pipe
          - Mixture too rich
          - Flooded float chamber
          - Air lock
          - Binding needle
      - No compression
        - Broken piston rings
        - Piston rings gummed
        - Broken piston, connecting rod or crankshaft
    - No spark at plug points
      - No spark at magneto
        - Breaker arm free
          - Sticking breaker arm
          - Contact points require attention
        - Spark at magneto
          - Failure in condenser
          - Failure of insulation
          - Dirty contact points
          - Faulty wiring
          - Dirty plug
          - Broken plug
          - Lead detached
          - Water short-circuits H.T. leads

- Engine will not run slowly
  - Petrol-oil mixture incorrect
  - Incorrect needle
  - Worn carburetor
  - Air leaks anywhere
  - Crankcase drain screw loose
  - Worn crankshaft bearings or leaky seals
  - Ignition too far advanced
  - Needs decarbonizing
  - Carburettor controls out of adjustment

Index

ACCELERATION, 60
Air cleaner, cleaning, 64
Air filter, 54
Armature, 18
  Siba Dynastart, 85
Armature plate, assembly, 37

BASEPLATE, 26
Battery, care of, 41
Blower cooling, 17
Bowden cable, lubricating, 57
Bulb replacement, 40

CABLE, adjustment of, 67
Carburettor—
  affixes, 54
  principle of, 42
  tuning, 51
  Type Junior 6/0(1F, 4F and 6F), 43
  Type S12 (4F, 6F, later), 46
  Type S19 (12D, 30C, 31C), 49
  Type S22 (2L, 3L, 2T, 3T), 52
  Type S24 (11D, 7E, 8E), 54
  Type S25, 25/S (12D, 30C and 31C), 54
  types, jets and needles, 55
Castrol oils, 62
Chaincase, lubricating oils, 62
Changing of gear, 67
Circlips, 72
Cleaning engine, 73
Clutch—
  adjustment of, 67, 69, 71
  use of, 61
Clutch case lubrication, 62
Clutch push rod (Mark 9E, 31C, 2L), 71
Contact breaker—
  adjustment of, 19
    Mark 2F, 20
  dismantling, 25
  Siba Dynastart, 85
Contact breaker gap, 22
Controls, 60
Control cable adjustment, 67

Crankcase draining, 66
Cycle of operations, 3
Cylinder—
  checking bore, 73
  removal of, 72

DECARBONIZING, 71
Diagrams, wiring—
  direct—
    6 volt, 10E, 2L, 34
    12 volt, 10E, 2L, 35
    4F, 6F, 30
    Marks 2T, 3T, 39
    rectifier 6 volt, 31A, 31C, 9E, 34
    Siba Dynastart, 88
Dipstick, check, 64
Direct type lighting set, 4F, 6F, 30
Dismantling—
  of magneto-generator (2L, 31A, 31C, 9E, 10C), 36
  of magneto-generator (4F, 6F), 29
Drip-feed oiling system, 56
Driving the cycle, 60
Dynastart, Siba, 85
  lighting, 88
  overhauling, 85

ELECTRIC lighting systems (see Lighting systems)
Energol oils, 62
Engines—
  98 c.c.—
    Midget and Junior, 7
    1F, 2F, 4F, 6F, 9
  122 c.c.—
    9D, 10D, 10
    12D, 11
  147–148 c.c., 29C, 30C, 12
  173 c.c., 2L, 13
  197 c.c., 6E, 7E, 8E, 9E, 13
  225 c.c., 1H, 14
  246 c.c., 2H, 31A, 15
  250 c.c., 2T, 15
  324 c.c., 3T, 16

Engine details, sketches—
9E, 2L, 31C, 75
4F, 6F, 77
2T, 3T, 79
cowled engine and starter, 80
Engine—
recommended oils, 62
running-in, 61
starting up, 58
stopping, 60
Engine lubrication, 56
Engine timing, 27
Esso oils, 62
Expander ring, 2

FAULT-finding charts, 90, 91, 92
Fault finding in Siba Dynastart, 87
Fitting cylinder and piston, 73
Flat-topped piston engines, 3
Flywheel—
refitting, 22
removal of, 21
timing, 22
Freeplay clutch lever, 70

GAP—
sparking plug, 81
contact breaker, 26
Gearbox lubrication, 57
Gearbox, recommended grades, 62
Gear cable adjustment, 67
Gear change, 67
Gear-change mechanism—
Mark 6F, 68
new patterns, 69
Gears, use of ratios, 60
Gudgeon pin, 2
removal of, 72

HAMMER-TIGHT spanner, 21, 22, 64

IGNITION—
timing, 23
retiming, 26

JETS, carburettor, 55
Junior 6/0, 43
S.12, 46
S.19, S.25, 49
S.22, 52

KIT, tool, 64

LEADS, magneto, 31
Lighting—
six volt set, 33
twelve volt set, 36
Lighting systems, 29
dismantling, 36
Mark 4F, 6F, 29
Mark 9F, 2L, 31C, 31A, 10E, 32
Mark 2T, 3T, 38
reassembling, 37
Siba Dynastart, 88
Lubricants, recommended, 62
Lubrication—
drip-feed system of, 56
grease, types of for, 62
of Bowden cables, 57, 63
of chaincase, 57, 63
of felt-pad, 27
Mark 2F, 20
of gearbox, 57
of machine, 63
of oil level plugs, 58, 59
of rocker arm pivot, 25
of speedometer drive, 57
oils, recommended grades of for—
engine, 62
gearbox, 57
petroil, system of, 56

MACHINE, lubricating, 63
Magneto—
Mark 4F, 6F, 29
Mark 9E, 2L, 31C, 31A, 10E, 32
principle of, 18
Magneto-adjusting cam, 29C, 30C, 19
Major overhauls, 81
Mobil oils, 62
Moving components, 1

NEEDLE, carburettor, 55
Junior 6/0, 43
S.12, 46
S.19, S.25, 49
S.22, 52
Needle taper in degrees, 55
Noise, 63

OIL level, dipstick check, 64
Oil level plugs, 58, 59

INDEX

Oils—
    grades for engine, 62
    grades for gearbox, 57
Overhauling, 64
    of Siba Dynastart, 85

PETROIL system, 56
Petrol consumption, 9, 10, 13, 14
Piston removal, 73
Plug chart, 83
Plug, diagnosis, 82
Plug gaps, 81
Plugs, types of, 83
Points, contact breaker, 20
Pre-mixed petroil, 56
Primary drive, adjustment of (Marks 9E, 2L, 31C), 69
Ports, cylinder, 4, 5

RACING engines, 16
Reassembling, magneto generators, 37
Reassembling Siba Dynastart, 87
Rectifier type lighting 4F, 6F, 30
Regent oils, 62
Removal of flywheel, 21
Replacement bulbs, 40
Rings, piston—
    checking, 73

Rings, piston—(*contd.*)
    removal of, 73
Routine attention, 64
Running-in, 61

SCRAMBLES, engines for, 16
Shell oils, 62
Siba Dynastart, 83
Sparking plug trouble-diagnosis, 82
Sparking plugs, 81
Sparking plugs, suitable, 83, 84
Speedo drive, lubrication, 57
Sports engines, 16
Starter, electric, 16
Starting up engine, 58
Stator, Siba Dynastart, 87
Stopping engine, 60
Strangler, 59

TIMING—
    of engine, 27
    of ignition, 22, 23
Tool kit, 64
Tracing troubles, 81
Tuning carburettors, 51

WIRING, diagrams, 30, 34, 35, 36, 39
    for Siba Dynastart, 88
Working parts, 1

AUTOBOOKS WORKSHOP MANUALS

ALFA ROMEO GIULIA 1300, 1600, 1750, 2000 1962-1978 WSM
BMW 1600 1966-1973 WSM
BMW 2000 & 2002 1966-1976 WSM
BMW 2500, 2800, 3.0 & 3.3 1968-1977 WSM
BMW 316, 320, 320i 1975-1977 WSM
BMW 518, 520, 520i 1973-1981 WSM
FIAT 1100, 1100D, 1100R & 1200 1957-1969 WSM
FIAT 124 1966-1974 WSM
FIAT 124 SPORT 1966-1975 WSM
FIAT 125 & 125 SPECIAL 1967-1973 WSM
FIAT 126, 126L, 126 DV, 126/650 & 126/650 DV 1972-1982 WSM
FIAT 127 SALOON, SPECIAL & SPORT, 900, 1050 1971-1981 WSM
FIAT 128 1969-1982 WSM
FIAT 1300, 1500 1961-1967 WSM
FIAT 131 MIRAFIORI 1975-1982 WSM
FIAT 132 1972-1982 WSM
FIAT 500 1957-1973 WSM
FIAT 600, 600D & MULTIPLA 1955-1969 WSM
FIAT 850 1964-1972 WSM
JAGUAR E-TYPE 1961-1972 WSM
JAGUAR MK 1, 2 1955-1969 WSM
JAGUAR S TYPE, 420 1963-1968 WSM
JAGUAR XK 120, 140, 150 MK 7, 8, 9 1948-1961 WSM
LAND ROVER 1, 2 1948-1961 WSM
MERCEDES-BENZ 190 1959-1968 WSM
MERCEDES-BENZ 220/8 1968-1972 WSM
MERCEDES-BENZ 220B 1959-1965 WSM
MERCEDES-BENZ 230 1963-1968 WSM
MERCEDES-BENZ 250 1968-1972 WSM
MERCEDES-BENZ 280 1968-1972 WSM
MG MIDGET TA-TF 1936-1955 WSM
MINI 1959-1980 WSM
MORRIS MINOR 1952-1971 WSM
PEUGEOT 404 1960-1975 WSM
PORSCHE 911 1964-1973 WSM
PORSCHE 911 1970-1977 WSM
RENAULT 16 1965-1979 WSM
RENAULT 8, 10, 1100 1962-1971 WSM
ROVER 3500, 3500S 1968-1976 WSM
SUNBEAM RAPIER, ALPINE 1955-1965 WSM
TRIUMPH SPITFIRE, GT6, VITESSE 1962-1968 WSM
TRIUMPH TR2, TR3, TR3A 1952-1962 WSM
TRIUMPH TR4, TR4A 1961-1967 WSM
VOLKSWAGEN BEETLE 1968-1977 WSM

VELOCEPRESS AUTOMOBILE BOOKS & MANUALS

ABARTH BUYERS GUIDE
AUSTIN-HEALEY 6-CYLINDER WSM
AUSTIN-HEALEY SPRITE & MG MIDGET 1958-1971 WSM
BMW 600 LIMOUSINE FACTORY WSM
BMW 600 LIMOUSINE OWNERS HAND BOOK & SERVICE MANUAL
BMW ISETTA FACTORY WSM
BOOK OF THE CARRERA PANAMERICANA - MEXICAN ROAD RACE
COMPLETE CATALOG OF JAPANESE MOTOR VEHICLES
CORVAIR 1960-1969 OWNERS WORKSHOP MANUAL
CORVETTE V8 1955-1962 OWNERS WORKSHOP MANUAL
DIALED IN - THE JAN OPPERMAN STORY
FERRARI 250/GT SERVICE AND MAINTENANCE
FERRARI 308 SERIES BUYER'S AND OWNER'S GUIDE
FERRARI BERLINETTA LUSSO
FERRARI BROCHURES AND SALES LITERATURE 1946-1967
FERRARI BROCHURES AND SALES LITERATURE 1968-1989
FERRARI GUIDE TO PERFORMANCE
FERRARI OPP, MAINTENANCE & SERVICE H/BOOKS 1948-1963
FERRARI OWNER'S HANDBOOK
FERRARI SERIAL NUMBERS PART I - ODD NUMBERS TO 21399
FERRARI SERIAL NUMBERS PART II - EVEN NUMBERS TO 1050
FERRARI SPYDER CALIFORNIA
FERRARI TUNING TIPS & MAINTENANCE TECHNIQUES
HENRY'S FABULOUS MODEL "A" FORD
HOW TO BUILD A FIBERGLASS CAR
HOW TO BUILD A RACING CAR
HOW TO RESTORE THE MODEL 'A' FORD
IF HEMINGWAY HAD WRITTEN A RACING NOVEL
JAGUAR E-TYPE 3.8 & 4.2 WSM
LE MANS 24 (THE BOOK THAT THE FILM WAS BASED ON)
MASERATI BROCHURES AND SALES LITERATURE
MASERATI OWNER'S HANDBOOK
METROPOLITAN FACTORY WSM
MGA & MGB OWNERS HANDBOOK & WSM
OBERT'S FIAT GUIDE
PERFORMANCE TUNING THE SUNBEAM TIGER
PORSCHE 356 1948-1965 WSM
PORSCHE 912 WSM
SOUPING THE VOLKSWAGEN
TRIUMPH TR2, TR3, TR4 1953-1965 WSM
TUNING FOR SPEED (P.E. IRVING)
VEDA ORR'S NEW REVISED HOT ROD PICTORIAL
VOLKSWAGEN TRANSPORTER, TRUCKS, STATION WAGONS WSM
VOLVO 1944-1968 ALL MODELS WSM
WEBER CARBURETORS (EMPHASIS ON ALFA & FIAT)

BROOKLANDS BOOKS & ROAD TEST PORTFOLIOS (RTP)

AC CARS 1904-2009
ALFA ROMEO 1920-1933 ROAD TEST PORTFOLIO
ALFA ROMEO 1934-1940 ROAD TEST PORTFOLIO
BRABHAM RALT HONDA THE RON TAURANAC STORY
BUGATTI TYPE 10 TO TYPE 40 ROAD TEST PORTFOLIO
BUGATTI TYPE 10 TO TYPE 251 ROAD TEST PORTFOLIO
BUGATTI TYPE 41 TO TYPE 55 ROAD TEST PORTFOLIO
BUGATTI TYPE 57 TO TYPE 251 ROAD TEST PORTFOLIO
DELAHAYE ROAD TEST PORTFOLIO
FERRARI ROAD CARS 1946-1956 ROAD TEST PORTFOLIO
FIAT 500 1936-1972 ROAD TEST PORTFOLIO
FIAT DINO ROAD TEST PORTFOLIO
HISPANO SUIZA ROAD TEST PORTFOLIO
HONDA ST1100/ST1300 PAN EUROPEAN 1990-2002 RTP
JAGUAR MK1 & MK2 ROAD TEST PORTFOLIO
LOTUS CORTINA ROAD TEST PORTFOLIO
MV AGUSTA F4 750 & 1000 1997-2007 ROAD TEST PORTFOLIO
TATRA CARS ROAD TEST PORTFOLIO

VELOCEPRESS MOTORCYCLE BOOKS & MANUALS

AJS SINGLES & TWINS 250cc THRU 1000cc 1932-1948 (BOOK OF)
AJS SINGLES 1955-65 350cc & 500cc (BOOK OF)
AJS SINGLES 1945-60 350cc & 500cc MODELS 16 & 18 (BOOK OF)
ARIEL 1939-1960 4 STROKE SINGLES (BOOK OF)
ARIEL LEADER & ARROW 1958-1964 (BOOK OF)
ARIEL MOTORCYCLES 1933-1951 WSM
ARIEL PREWAR MODELS 1932-1939 (BOOK OF)
BMW M/CYCLES R26 R27 (1956-1967) FACTORY WSM
BMW M/CYCLES R50 R50S R60 R69S (1955-1969) FACTORY WSM
BSA BANTAM (BOOK OF)
BSA ALL FOUR-STROKE SINGLES & V-TWINS 1936-1952 (BOOK OF)
BSA OHV & SV SINGLES - 250cc 1954-1970 (BOOK OF)
BSA OHV & SV SINGLES 1945-54 250-600cc (BOOK OF)
BSA OHV SINGLES 350 & 500cc 1955-1967 (BOOK OF)
BSA PRE-WAR MODELS TO 1939 (BOOK OF)
BSA TWINS 1948-1962 (BOOK OF)
BSA TWINS 1962-1969 (SECOND BOOK OF)
CATALOG OF BRITISH MOTORCYCLES (1951 MODELS)
DOUGLAS PRE-WAR ALL MODELS 1929-1939 (BOOK OF)
DOUGLAS POST-WAR ALL MODELS 1948-1957 FACTORY WSM
DUCATI 160cc, 250 & 350cc OHC MODELS FACTORY WSM
HONDA 50 ALL MODELS UP TO 1970 INC MONKEY & TRAIL (BOOK OF)
HONDA 90 ALL MODELS UP TO 1966 (BOOK OF)
HONDA MOTORCYCLES 125-150 TWINS C/CS/CB/CA WSM
HONDA MOTORCYCLES 250-305 TWINS C/CS/CB WSM
HONDA MOTORCYCLES C100 SUPER CUB WSM
HONDA MOTORCYCLES C110 SPORT CUB 1962-1969 WSM
HONDA TWINS & SINGLES 50cc THRU 305cc 1960-1966 (BOOK OF)
HONDA TWINS ALL MODELS 125cc THRU 450cc UP TO 1968 (BOOK OF)
INDIAN PONYBIKE, BOY RACER & PAPOOSE ILL PARTS LIST & SALES LIT
LAMBRETTA ALL 125 & 150cc MODELS 1947-1957 (BOOK OF)
LAMBRETTA LI & TV MODELS 1957-1970 (SECOND BOOK OF)
MATCHLESS 350 & 500cc SINGLES 1945-1956 (BOOK OF)
MATCHLESS 350 & 500cc SINGLES 1955-1966 (BOOK OF)
NORTON 1932-1947 (BOOK OF)
NORTON 1938-1956 (BOOK OF)
NORTON DOMINATOR TWINS 1955-1965 (BOOK OF)
NORTON MODELS 19, 50 & ES2 1955-1963 (BOOK OF)
NORTON MOTORCYCLES 1957-1970 FACTORY WSM
NORTON PREWAR MODELS 1932-1939 (BOOK OF)
NSU QUICKLY ALL MODELS 1953-1963 (BOOK OF)
ROYAL ENFIELD SINGLES & V TWINS 1937-1953 (BOOK OF)
ROYAL ENFIELD SINGLES 1946-1962 (BOOK OF)
ROYAL ENFIELD 736cc INTERCEPTOR FACTORY WSM
ROYAL ENFIELD 250cc & 350cc SINGLES 1958-1966 (SECOND BOOK OF)
SUZUKI 50cc & 80cc UP TO 1966 (BOOK OF)
SUZUKI T10 1963-1967 FACTORY WSM
SUZUKI T20 & T200 1965-1969 FACTORY WSM
TRIUMPH PRE-WAR MOTORCYCLE 1935-1939 (BOOK OF)
TRIUMPH MOTORCYCLES 1937-1951 WSM
TRIUMPH MOTORCYCLES 1945-1955 FACTORY WSM
TRIUMPH TWINS 1956-1969 (BOOK OF)
VELOCETTE ALL SINGLES & TWINS 1925-1970 (BOOK OF)
VESPA 1951-1961 (BOOK OF)
VESPA 125 & 150cc & GS MODELS 1955-1963 (SECOND BOOK OF)
VESPA 90, 125 & 150cc 1963-1972 (THIRD BOOK OF)
VESPA GS & SS 1955-1968 (BOOK OF)
VILLIERS ENGINE (BOOK OF)
VINCENT MOTORCYCLES 1935-1955 WSM

PLEASE VISIT OUR WEBSITE
www.VelocePress.com
FOR A DETAILED DESCRIPTION
OF ANY OF THESE TITLES

www.ingramcontent.com/pod-product-compliance
Lightning Source LLC
Chambersburg PA
CBHW070600170426
43201CB00012B/1889